Rescued by...

Excel for Windows

Allen L. Wyatt

JAMSA
P · R · E · S · S
...a computer user's best friend

a division of Kris Jamsa Software, Inc.

Published by
Jamsa Press
2821 High Sail Ct.
Las Vegas, NV 89117
U.S.A.

For information about the translation or distribution of any Jamsa Press book, please write to Jamsa Press at the address listed above.

Rescued by Excel for Windows

Printed in the United States of America.
98765432

ISBN 0-9635851-8-5

Publisher
  Debbie Jamsa

Copy Editor
  Paul Medoff

Composition
  Kevin Hutchinson
  Phil Schmauder

Cover Design
  Jeff Wolfley & Associates

Layout Design
  Discovery Computing, Inc.

Technical Editor
  Ken Cope

Illustrator
  Phil Schmauder

Indexer
  Ken Cope

Cover Photograph
  O'Gara/Bissell

Table of Contents

Learning the Ropes

Section One

Excel is a powerful spreadsheet program that makes working with numbers quick and easy. Before you can start using Excel effectively, however, you must learn the basics—the skills that act as a foundation for everything you do in the program. This section will provide you with the information you need to build a firm foundation. Here you will learn how to start and end the program, as well as how to get help when you need it. You will learn about the tools used in Excel and how to get around in your workbook. By the time you finish this section, you will have mastered many of the skills necessary to grow and develop effectively with Excel.

Lesson 1 *Starting and Ending Excel*

Lesson 2 *Getting Help When You Need It*

Lesson 3 *Positioning Excel*

Lesson 4 *The Excel Environment*

Lesson 5 *How to Get Around in Excel*

Lesson 1

Starting and Ending Excel

If you have been using Windows for any time, there is a good chance you will feel right at home with Excel. This spreadsheet program makes full use of all the features of Windows, including menus, buttons, and bars. In this lesson you will learn how to

- Start Excel

- Use Excel menus

- Select menus and options

- Exit Excel

STARTING EXCEL

To start Excel, you must first be in the Windows Program Manager. The Program Manager is where you will most likely start all of your Windows programs; it should look something like Figure 1.1.

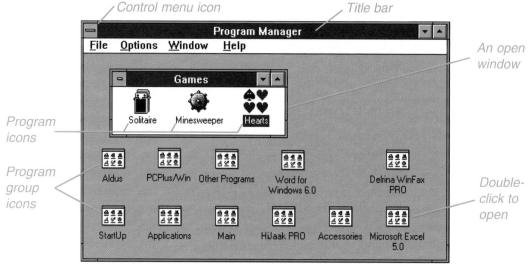

Figure 1.1 The Windows Program Manager.

Notice that the title bar, at the top of the window, says **Program Manager**. This window contains both *icons* (little pictures) that represent *program groups* and open windows (program groups whose windows have been opened), which contain icons that represent programs. One of the program groups or windows on your screen should be titled **Excel**. (This title might be followed by a version number, such as **Excel 5.0**, or it might appear as **Microsoft Excel 5.0**.) If this program group is an icon, double-click on the icon with the mouse. *Double-click* means to press the left mouse button twice in quick succession. When you do this properly, the program group icon will be expanded to an open window, as shown in Figure 1.2.

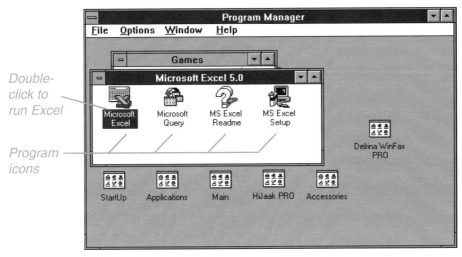

Figure 1.2 The Excel program group.

Notice that the program group window contains at least two *program icons*—**Microsoft Excel** and **Microsoft Excel Setup**—but there could be more.

To start Excel, simply double-click on the Microsoft Excel icon; the program will start, and you will see the Microsoft Excel program window, as shown in Figure 1.3.

Your screen might differ a little, depending on the options you have set. Over the course of this book you will learn how to use and set the options that control how your screen looks. One thing that should be the same, regardless of the actual appearance of your screen, is the menu bar at the top of the Microsoft Excel window.

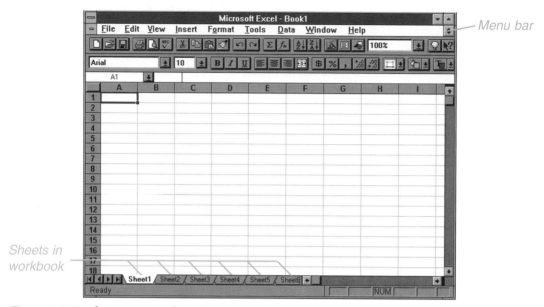

Menu bar

Sheets in workbook

Figure 1.3 Excel program window when you first start the program.

At its simplest, Excel is a program that allows you to work with workbooks and sheets. A *workbook* is nothing more than a collection of sheets, and *sheets* are nothing more than what you may already know as spreadsheet files. Sheets generally contain text, numbers, and formulas, but they can contain other objects, as well. You will learn about some of these other objects later in this book.

When you start Excel, it typically starts with a brand new workbook already loaded. If this happens, your menu will appear as previously shown, and you will see an open workbook ready for you to enter information. If your menu bar appears shorter, like this:

Menu bar if no worksheet open

you will need to either create a workbook or load an existing one (Lesson 12). To create a workbook, you will need to use the menu.

USING EXCEL MENUS

There are two ways you can use a menu. The first is to point the mouse pointer to the menu you want to use and click on the left mouse button. When the menu *drops down* from the menu bar, as shown in Figure 1.4, you can either double-click on the option you want or click once on the option, moving the highlight to it, and press ENTER.

The other method is to use the keyboard. To do this, you hold down the ALT key and press the underlined letter in the menu name. For instance, to use the File menu, you would press ALT-F. The menu will then drop down from the bar, as shown in Figure 1.4, and you can either press the underlined letter of the option you want or move the highlight to option you want with the arrow keys and press ENTER.

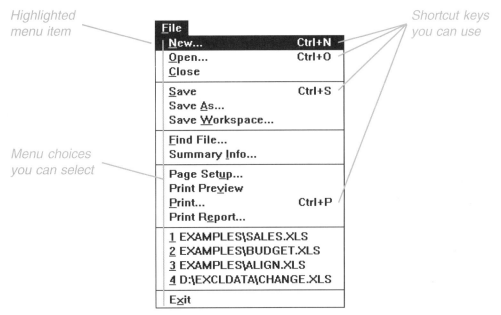

Figure 1.4 The File menu.

Note that, in the case of the File menu, there are many choices you can make. Not every menu has lots of different choices; some have only a few. The option names are always on the left side of the menu, and a *shortcut keypress* (if there is one) is displayed at the right side. These shortcut keys indicate ways you can access the option without using the menu. For example, to open an existing workbook you can press CTRL-O directly, without having to pull down the File menu.

Excel is a very powerful program that allows you to change just about everything to customize the program to how you work. This includes the ability to change the menus. If your program has not been customized extensively, there are nine menus that you can use to execute the commands that control the program and affect your worksheet. These are shown in Table 1.1.

Menu	Function
File	Allows you to perform file-related activities, including printing.
Edit	Used to edit, search, replace, and link text.
View	Defines a few options concerning how you want Excel to appear for you.
Insert	Allows you to insert information into your worksheet.
Format	Allows you to format (change the appearance of) information in your worksheet.
Tools	Provides access to special functions and tools, such as macros.
Data	Allows you to work with the information in your workbook as if it were a database or to access other database functions.
Window	If you have multiple worksheets open at once (see Section 6, "Excel Shortcuts,"), this menu allows you to choose how you view the various worksheets.
Help	Allows you to get either general or specific help.

Table 1.1 The Excel for Windows menus.

As you begin to work with Excel, there is no better way to get used to the program than to start working with the menus. Go ahead—select various menus and menu options. It won't hurt a thing, and you will begin to see some of what Excel can do for you.

ENDING EXCEL

When you have finished using Excel, you can quickly and easily exit the program. Remember when you viewed the File menu earlier in this lesson? One of the options from that menu was **Exit**. This option allows you to exit the program and return to the Program Manager. You can also, however, double-click on the Control menu icon (⊟), which is located in the upper-left corner of the window.

If you prefer using the keyboard, pressing ALT-F4 also allows you to leave the program. When you leave, Excel might display the dialog box shown in Figure 1.5:

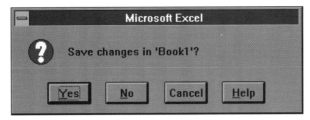

Figure 1.5 *Click Yes to save the worksheet.*

This simply means that you have made some changes to the worksheet in memory, and Excel wants to find out if you want them saved before you leave the program. Once you leave the program, you cannot recover any information that was not saved. If you want to learn more about saving information in a file, refer to Lesson 11, "Saving Your Sheet."

WHAT YOU NEED TO KNOW

In this lesson you have had your first encounter with Excel. Since this is the first lesson, important concepts have been covered. You should know how to do the following:

☑ You start Excel by using the mouse to double-click on the Microsoft Excel program icon.

☑ Many Excel commands are accessed through pull-down menus. You access these menus by using the mouse to click on one of the choices on the menu bar at the top of the screen.

☑ When you want to exit Excel, the easiest way is to use the mouse to double-click on the Control menu icon in the upper left corner of the Excel program window.

If you are still unclear on any of these items, read through the lesson again before moving on. Starting Excel, using the menus, and ending Excel are all integral to everything else you do in the program.

In the next lesson you will learn how to get Excel help when you need it.

Lesson 2

Getting Help When You Need It

In Lesson 1 you learned how you can start and end Excel. Once you are working with Excel, however, there might be times when you need a little help. This is particularly true if you are just starting out with Excel or you are using a command that you don't use often.

Excel provides a great help system. This help system works basically the same as the help system in any other Windows program. In this lesson you will learn the following:

- How to access the help system
- What the parts of the Help window are and how they work
- How to access related help topics through the use of interactive links
- How to see definitions of key terms
- How to move through the help system
- How to search for a help topic
- How to get context-sensitive help
- How to keep the Help window displayed
- How to use the TipWizard

ACCESSING HELP

In Lesson 1 you learned about the menu system in Excel. Take another look at the menu bar:

Help menu choice ⎯⎯⎯⎤

File	**Edit**	**View**	**Insert**	**Format**	**Tools**	**Data**	**Window**	**Help**

At the very right side of the menu bar is a choice labeled **Help**. If you choose this menu, you will see a list of different types of help you can receive, as shown in Figure 2.1.

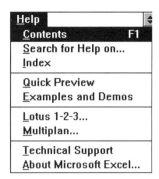

Figure 2.1 The Help menu.

The first three menu choices are covered later in this lesson The fourth through seventh choices from the Help menu allow you to access various tutorials about how to use Excel. These will come in handy when you have the time to use them; particularly if you are first learning the program.

The eighth choice, Technical Support, is used when you need to call Microsoft because you have a problem that you cannot resolve in any other way, for instance, if your program simply refuses to act as it should or if you are interested in receiving an update. The final help choice, About Microsoft Excel, is also helpful if you call Microsoft for support. When you choose this item, you will see a dialog box similar to the one shown in Figure 2.2.

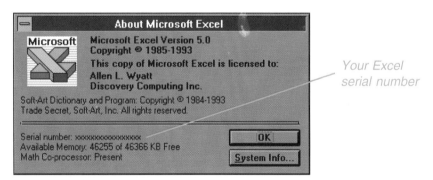

Figure 2.2 The About Microsoft Excel dialog box.

This provides information about your copy of Excel. It even includes your serial number, which will be needed any time you talk to a technical support person at Microsoft. When you have finished viewing the About dialog box, click on ⬛ OK.

Select the Contents option from the Help menu. When you do, you will see the Help window appear, as shown in Figure 2.3.

Menu bar

Button bar

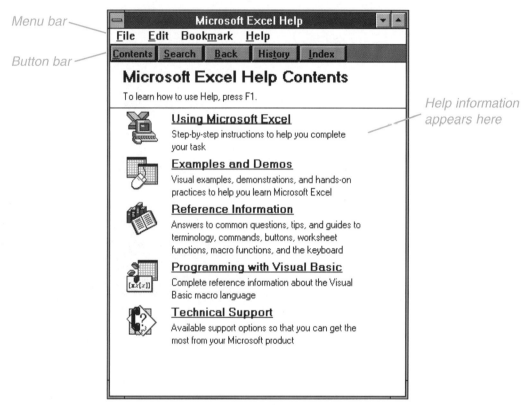

Help information appears here

Figure 2.3 *The Help window.*

The actual appearance of your Help window might be different. For instance, it might be wider or shorter, or it might be very small. This is because, as you adjust the size of the Help window (as well as its position), it is remembered from one help session to another. The size and position of the window you see currently is the same as when the Help window was last displayed.

There are three parts to a Help window. The first is the menu, which offers four choices. What these choices do is not necessarily important to getting help about a topic. They are provided for those people who want to load different help files or make changes to the help file currently being used.

The second part of the Help window is the button bar. It appears directly beneath the menu. There are four buttons on this bar; each will be explained later in this lesson.

Finally, there is the body of the Help window. This is where you can see information about a topic. It is in this area where you will get the most information about the subject. You can scroll through this window as you would through any other window (see Lesson 5).

When you have finished using the help system, you can close window by double-clicking on the Control menu icon (⊟) in the upper-left corner of the Help window. You can also choose the Exit option from the File menu of the Help window.

HELP IS INTERACTIVE

The help files used by Excel are completely interactive. This means you can quickly access different parts of a help file. For instance, take another look at the help screen that is displayed when you select Contents from the Help menu (it was shown in Figure 2.3).

Notice that there are many terms on the screen, related to the original topic, that are underlined. These are *interactive links*. As you move the mouse pointer over these terms, it changes to a hand. This means you can click the left mouse button to receive help related to that item.

As you move from screen to screen, you can use the Back button on the button bar to get back to the previous screen. This button allows you to step back one screen at a time. If you want to step back more than one screen, you can click on the History button. When you do, you will see a dialog box that contains a list of all the help topics you have viewed, as shown in Figure 2.4:

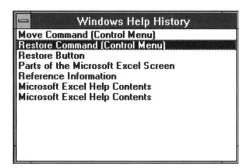

Figure 2.4 The Help History dialog box.

You can select any of the listed topics by using the mouse to double-click on the topic. If you decide you want to jump back to the contents for the current help file (this is the display that appears when you first select Help Index from the Help menu), all you need to do is click on the Contents button.

There is another feature of the help system of which you should be aware. This is the glossary terms. The people who developed Excel understand that there may be terminology used that is new or unusual to you. If you see a term that is underlined with a dashed line, you can view a definition of that term by clicking on it. For instance, the help screen shown in Figure 2.5 shows both interactive links (terms with a solid underline) and glossary terms (terms with a dashed underline).

Figure 2.5 Help screen, showing interactive links and glossary terms.

SEARCHING FOR A TOPIC

While you can select a general help topic from the Contents screen, it is often more productive to jump directly to the topic you want to view. This is done by clicking on the Search button. When you do, you will see the Search dialog box, shown in Figure 2.6.

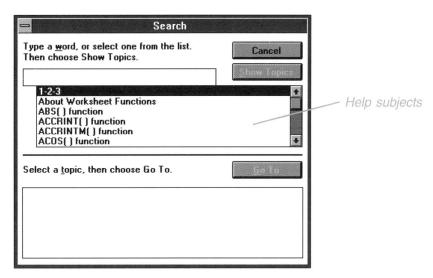

Figure 2.6 *The Search dialog box.*

The Search dialog box is divided into two sections. In the top section is a list of general subject areas. You can either scroll through the list, using the mouse, or you can start to type the name of the topic you want. As you type, the subject window displays the first subject that most closely matches what you are typing. When you have selected a subject, you can click on the [Show Topics] button, and you will see a list of topics for that subject area. These are displayed in the box at the bottom of the Search dialog box, as shown in Figure 2.7.

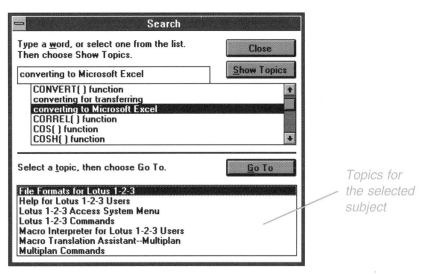

Figure 2.7 *The Search dialog box, showing topics.*

Select one of the topics you want to view. If you double-click on the topic, you will see the help information on that topic right away. If you would rather, you can simply select the topic and then click on the ▓ Go To ▓ button.

HELP ON A MENU TOPIC

Excel allows you to access the help system by pressing the **F1** key at any time. When you do, Excel will attempt to display help that is appropriate to the task you are performing. This is referred to as *context-sensitive* help, meaning that help is displayed based on the context in which you request the help.

For instance, if you need help concerning clearing information, all you need to do is highlight the Clear option from the Edit menu and press **F1**. The Help system is displayed, with the appropriate help information.

Alternatively, you can click on the inquiry tool (▓) on the Excel toolbar (the toolbar is discussed in more depth in Lesson 4). When you do, the mouse cursor changes shape, becoming a help pointer. The help pointer looks like this:

— Help pointer

When you select a function or menu choice using this help pointer, Excel will display help about that topic instead of executing the command or menu choice. This technique will work for any menu item, and during the middle of many other operations you may perform in Excel.

KEEPING HELP DISPLAYED

The help system is simply another Windows program. When you are using help, you normally cannot work on your Excel document at the same time. If you do, the Help window will disappear behind the window used by Excel. However, the help system has a feature that allows you to keep the Help window displayed at all times. If you select the Always on Top option from the Help menu (the one in the Help window), you can work on your document while the Help window is displayed. This is great for when you are following a series of steps that may be displayed in the Help window.

USING THE TIP WIZARD

Excel includes a unique feature that allows you to improve your skills as you use the program. Granted, you will improve simply by getting practice in using Excel, but the TipWizard actually analyzes how you do your work with Excel, and then offers suggestions on how to perform the same operations quicker or easier. Thus, it doesn't teach you how to do things, but how to do things better.

Using the TipWizard is very easy. All you need to do is click on the 💡 tool on the standard toolbar. You will then see the TipWizard toolbar appear, as shown in Figure 2.8. (You will learn more about toolbars in Lesson 4, "The Excel Environment," and Lesson 30, "Using Toolbars.")

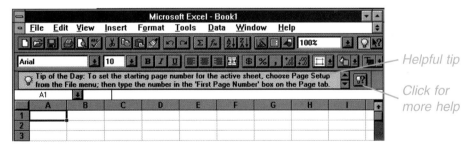

Figure 2.8 *The TipWizard toolbar.*

When you first use the TipWizard, your screen will not appear the same; you will probably not see the same tip. This is because when you first turn on the TipWizard, it displays a random tip of the day. As you begin to work, however, the TipWizard performs its analysis and displays tips that will help you work quicker, easier, or more efficiently. If you decide you later want to turn the TipWizard off, all you need to do is again click on the 💡 tool.

WHAT YOU NEED TO KNOW

Excel provides a full-featured help system that can answer many questions you might have about how the program works. After working through this lesson, you should have a pretty good grip on how to use the help system. In particular, you should know the following:

- ☑ You can access extensive on-line help by using the pull-down Help menu and then selecting one of the menu choices.

- ☑ The help system uses interactive links that allow you to review related help topics. These topics are typically shown on-screen with a solid underline. Using the mouse to click on the topic displays help for that topic.

- ☑ You can see definitions for any term that has a dotted underline. This is done by using the mouse to click on the term.

- ☑ The help system contains its own button bar that aids you in moving through the help system.

- ☑ Clicking on the Search button allows you to jump to help for any topic you desire.

- ☑ Through the use of the ▶? tool (on the standard toolbar) you can get context-sensitive help for any Excel command.

- ☑ The TipWizard can be used to help analyze the way you work. It provides information on how to complete tasks quicker and easier.

As you are working with Excel, you will find yourself accessing the help system often. As you learn different parts of the program, you might have to use it less and less, but there will still be times you will need help for commands and procedures that you do not use daily.

In the next lesson you will learn about the different types of windows and how to move and resize a window.

Lesson 3

Positioning Excel

Excel implements the user interface of Windows very effectively. A *user interface* defines how a program appears and interacts with you, the user. You have undoubtedly noticed that this user interface centers on using windows to display information. For the most part, you have control over where and how those windows are displayed. In this lesson you will learn the following information related to Excel:

- The different types of windows used in Windows
- How to control the size of a window
- How to adjust the position of window borders
- How to move a window

UNDERSTANDING DIFFERENT WINDOWS

Windows (not just Excel) uses two different types of windows. *Program windows* are used by programs; *document windows* are used to display information within program windows. Generally, document windows are used to contain data used by the program you are running (in this case, the document windows contain workbooks and sheets). These two types of windows can typically be told apart by the presence of a menu bar. Program windows, the vast majority of times, have menu bars, and document windows do not.

In Excel, there is only one program window (it contains the menu bar for the Excel program), but there can be multiple document windows. In Lesson 32 you will learn how you can work with more than one document window at a time. I bring this up now so you can understand the relationship between the different windows with which you will be working.

CONTROLLING THE WINDOW SIZE

Both document windows and program windows are controlled in the same manner. You can adjust the size of both types of windows using the same techniques.

There are three types of sizes for any window. The first is *minimized*. In this condition, a window is reduced to the size of an icon. These are the same type of icons you see when you are working with the Program Manager. The second is *maximized*. In this condition, a window occupies all of the available screen space. If you are working exclusively with one program, you will probably want to maximize its program window. This provides the largest amount of workspace. The third window condition is somewhere in between, *restored*. In this condition you can see other windows on your screen besides the one in which you are working.

So how do you control the size of a window? The easiest method is to use the sizing buttons in the upper-right corner of a window. There are three types of buttons, shown in Table 3.1:

Button	Function
▲	Maximizes the window; it becomes as large as possible, covering your entire screen.
▼	Minimizes the window, reducing it to the size of an icon. This does not end the program, it simply puts the program aside so you can work on other tasks. Your documents are still available within the program. To open the window again, simply double-click on the icon.
↕	This is referred to as the *restore button*. It appears only when a window is maximized, and is used to return a window to its "in-between" size.

Table 3.1 Window sizing buttons.

You should note that not all windows can be minimized. Program windows can, however it is up to the program whether document windows can be minimized.

Take another look at the windows in your Excel environment. The sizing buttons might appear like this:

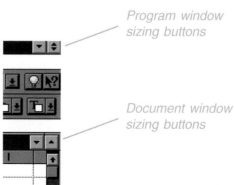

Program window
sizing buttons

Document window
sizing buttons

The lower maximize button is associated with your Excel document; it is part of the document window. If you click on this button, the document window is enlarged, and the sizing buttons become this:

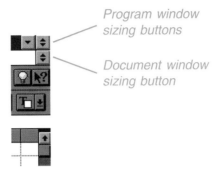

*Program window
sizing buttons*

*Document window
sizing button*

The top two sizing buttons control the program window, while the lower one still controls the size of the document window. If you click on the restore button for the document window (that's the lower button), the document window is restored to its smaller size.

Go ahead and restore the size of the document window. Notice that the window no longer fills up the entire program window used by Excel. This prepares you for the next technique you should learn—changing the overall size of a window.

You already know how to make a window as small as possible (minimizing) and how to make one as large as possible (maximizing), but you can also adjust the overall size of the window manually. This is done by moving the window borders. Take a look at the borders of your windows. They should be fairly thin, and they will probably be a different color than other parts of your screen. For instance, in the following corner of a worksheet (a document window), the border is a dark green:

Window border

As you move the mouse cursor so it is positioned over the border, notice that it changes:

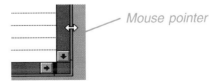

Mouse pointer

This is what it looks like when you move the mouse cursor to either of the side borders. The double arrows indicate the directions in which you can move the border. If move it to the top or bottom border, the arrows will point up and down. If you move it to a corner, they will point diagonally, like this:

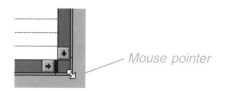

Mouse pointer

This indicates you can affect two borders at one time—one horizontal and one vertical. When the mouse cursor changes to any of these double arrows, you can move the borders. All you need to do is hold down the left mouse button and move the mouse. As you do, the border moves with the mouse cursor. You are *dragging* the border. When you are pleased with the positioning of the border, simply release the mouse button. The border will stay where you released the button.

QUICK REVIEW

Controlling and sizing windows within Excel is done in the same manner as in other Windows programs. The majority of your sizing needs are handled through three different buttons which appear int he upper right corner of any window:

- The minimize button (▼) allows you to reduce an open window to the size of an icon.

- The maximize button (▲) allows you to expand a window so it fills the entire screen.

- The restore button (↕) allows you to reduce the size of a window to an "in-between" size.

Additional sizing can be performed by moving the mouse cursor over a window border, clicking and holding the left mouse button, and moving the border to reflect the desired window size.

CONTROLLING THE WINDOW POSITION

Moving a window is even easier than changing window size. To move a window, simply drag it by its title bar. Point the mouse pointer at the window's title bar. (If you need a refresher on where the title bar is located, refer to Figure 1.1 in Lesson 1.) Then click and hold the left mouse button. As you move the mouse, the window border will move. When you release the mouse button, the window is redrawn at the place where you released the button. You can move windows and resize them as you please.

WHAT YOU NEED TO KNOW

One of the benefits of working in the Windows environment is that you can determine how your screen looks. You can rearrange and resize windows as you desire, resulting in a workspace that reflects how you need to work. As you finish this lesson, you should have learned the following information:

- ☑ Windows uses different types of windows; both document and program windows. Each has a different purpose, but can be controlled in the same manner.

- ☑ You can use the window control buttons in the upper right corner of any window to control general window size.

- ☑ You can change the size of windows by adjusting the position of individual window borders.

- ☑ You can reposition a window by clicking on the title bar and dragging the window to a new position.

In the next lesson you will learn about the Excel environment, including menus, toolbars, the formula bar, sheet tabs, and the status bar.

Lesson 4

The Excel Environment

As you have already learned, Excel provides a rich environment that allows you to tailor the program to how you work, instead of the other way around. In earlier lessons you performed some of this tailoring. For instance, you learned how to adjust window sizes. As you work through this book you will always be learning new ways to change what Excel does. Before you can do that, however, you must learn more about the actual Excel environment. In this lesson you will learn about various parts of the environment, including:

- What the toolbars are and how they are used

- What the formula bar can be used for

- How the sheet tabs work

- Information provided on the status bar

Take a look at your Excel program window, as shown in Figure 4.1.

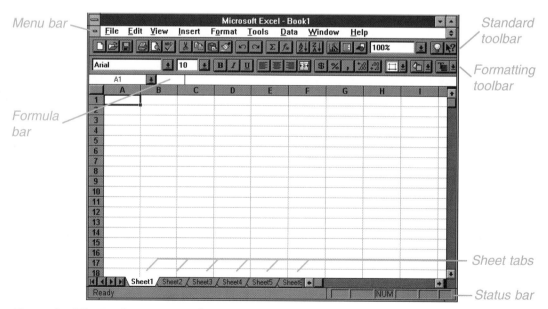

Figure 4.1 The Excel program window.

Notice the six elements pointed out on the screen. These elements might not all be visible on your screen, however. The elements that can be displayed (and are shown in this illustration) are, from top to bottom:

- The menu bar
- The standard toolbar
- The formatting toolbar
- The formula bar
- The sheet tabs
- The status bar

The first three items are located at the top of the screen; the status bar is located at the bottom. The menu bar is always visible and cannot be turned off. You learned about how to use the menus in Lesson 1. In this lesson you will learn about each of the other elements in the Excel environment.

UNDERSTANDING TOOLBARS

In Excel, a *toolbar* contains a series of buttons, each of which represents a tool. Excel supports multiple toolbars for a variety of purposes. For instance, in Figure 4.1 there are two toolbars displayed at the top of the screen. One of these toolbars is referred to as the *standard toolbar,* and the other as the *formatting toolbar.* The first toolbar is used for standard functions, and the other is used for formatting. Other toolbars are available for special purposes, such as drawing, charting, and creating macros.

If you cannot see any toolbars on your screen, this is because they are turned off. If you want to display a toolbar, choose Toolbars from the View menu. When you do, you will see the Toolbars dialog box, as shown in Figure 4.2.

Excel has 13 predefined toolbars from which you can choose. You can display any or all of the toolbars. The check box to the left of the toolbar name indicates whether the toolbar is displayed. In Figure 4.2, you can tell that only the standard and formatting toolbars are displayed. These are the two toolbars displayed when Excel is first started.

Different toolbars will be used throughout this book for different purposes. Whenever a different toolbar is required, this will be indicated. For instance, you learned about the TipWizard toolbar in Lesson 2. For most purposes, however, the standard and formatting toolbars will do the trick. To follow along with the examples in this book, you should have at least these toolbars displayed.

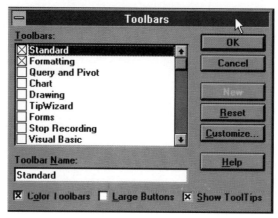

Figure 4.2 The Toolbars dialog box.

THE STANDARD TOOLBAR

Normally, there are 22 tools (buttons) on the standard toolbar. You might actually have more or fewer tools than this, however, based on the toolbars selected and the way they have been customized Assuming that the standard toolbar is displayed and it has not been changed by anyone, Table 4.1 shows what each tool represents.

Button	Function
	Creates a new workbook
	Allows you to load (open) a workbook; same as choosing Open from the File menu
	Saves the current workbook to disk; same as choosing Save from the File menu
	Prints a single copy of your workbook
	Allows you to preview what your workbook will look like when it is printed; same as choosing Print Preview from the File menu
	Starts the spelling checker; same as choosing Spelling from the Tools menu
	Cuts the selection, removing it from the sheet and placing it in the Clipboard
	Copies the selection from the sheet to the Clipboard

Table 4.1 Tools available on the standard toolbar. (continued on next page)

Button	Function
	Pastes the contents of the Clipboard onto the sheet
	Initiates the format painter, which allows you to copy and paste formats
	Allows you to undo the last action or command; same as choosing Undo from the Edit menu
	Allows you to redo the last action or command; same as choosing Repeat from the Edit menu
	Initiates use of the SUM function
	Starts the function wizard for help in using functions; same as selecting Function from the Insert menu
	Sorts in ascending order
	Sorts in descending order
	Allows you to create or edit a chart
	Allows you to add a floating text box to your sheet
	Displays or hides the drawing toolbar
100%	Controls the zoom magnification; similar to choosing Zoom from the View menu
	Turns on or off the TipWizard
	Inquiry tool—allows you to point to an item on the screen and receive help or display information about it

Table 4.1 Tools available on the standard toolbar. (continued from previous page)

As you work with the toolbars, you will come to appreciate the way they can save you time and effort. The tools are always handy, always available on the screen. You will not learn in-depth information about individual tools in this lesson, however. Instead, you will learn about them throughout this book.

THE FORMATTING TOOLBAR

The formatting toolbar is primarily used for formatting information appearing in your workbook. It appears directly beneath the standard toolbar, as shown in Figure 4.1. Make sure that the formatting toolbar is turned on for the examples used in this book.

The formatting toolbar has both buttons and selection lists. Each of these indicates the formatting applied to text and allows you to change that formatting. Table 4.2 explains each of the sections of the unmodified formatting toolbar.

Button	Function
Arial ⬇	Shows which font is applied to the selected characters. See Lesson 15 for more information on fonts.
10 ⬇	Shows the size of the font applied to the selected characters. See Lesson 15 for more information on fonts.
B *I* U	Indicates whether the selected text is bold, italic, or underlined. Any or all of these buttons can be selected to change how characters look. If the selected text includes the attribute, the appropriate button looks like it has been depressed (**B**).
≣ ≣ ≣ ≣	Changes the alignment of information within cells. The buttons align information within the cells left, center, right, and across a range of cells.
$	Applies a currency style to the selected cells.
%	Applies a percent style to the selected cells.
,	Applies a number style with commas to selected cells.
+.0 .00	Increases the number of decimal positions in a cell.
.00 +.0	Decreases the number of decimal positions in a cell.
⬚ ⬇	Applies borders to a range of cells.
⬛ ⬇	Applies color to the selected cells.
⬛ ⬇	Applies color to the selected text.

Table 4.2 *Tools available on the formatting toolbar.*

Formatting is a rather extensive topic in Excel for Windows because the program allows you to perform many different types of formatting functions. Section 3 provides you with complete information about formatting your workbook.

QUICK REVIEW

Excel provides two toolbars which are typically displayed at all times. The standard toolbar provides access to common commands and features, while the formatting toolbar allows you to quickly add formatting to information in your sheet. You can turn toolbars on and off by using the Toolbar option from the View menu.

The lessons in this book assume you will have both the standard and formatting toolbars displayed at all times.

THE FORMULA BAR

The formula bar appears just below the standard toolbar and is used to indicate the contents and status of the currently selected part of the worksheet. If you cannot see the formula bar, it is because it has been turned off. To turn it on, select Options from the Tools menu. When you do, you will see the Options dialog box, shown in Figure 4.3.

View file card

Controls formula bar

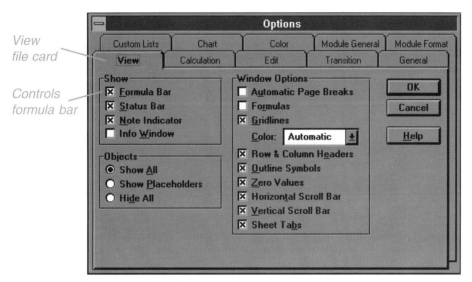

Figure 4.3 *The Options dialog box.*

This dialog box is used extensively in customizing Excel. Notice at the top of the dialog box there are ten tabs indicating different "file cards," which control the options displayed. If you see the Options dialog box, but it does not appear as shown in Figure 4.3, make sure that you select the View file card.

If an × appears to the left of the *Formula Bar* option on this dialog box, then the formula bar should appear in the Excel program window. If the × does not appear, then click on the Formula Bar option until it does. When you are satisfied with the setting, click on the ▓OK▓ button.

At the left side of the formula bar are the coordinates of the active cell. For instance, if the formula bar says A4, the cell at column A, row 4 is selected. The right side of the formula bar is information about the contents of the cell.

When you enter information into a worksheet, this information first appears on the formula bar. It is not placed in a cell until you press ENTER. You will learn about and use the formula bar extensively as you work through this book.

THE SHEET TABS

In earlier lessons you learned that a workbook is made up of individual sheets. Each of these sheets can be displayed, and information within the sheet can be updated and manipulated. The main tool you use to control which sheet is displayed is the row of *sheet tabs*, located at the bottom of an Excel document window:

If you cannot see the sheet tabs, it is because they are not turned on. To control whether the sheet tabs are displayed, choose Options from the Tools menu. When you do, you will see the Options dialog box, shown in Figure 4.4. Make sure the View file card is displayed.

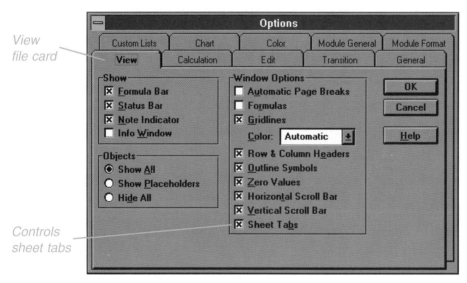

Figure 4.4 The Options dialog box.

To display the sheet tabs, make sure the Sheet Tabs option is enabled. While it is not essential that the sheet tabs be displayed, it makes it easier for you to control which sheet is displayed. It is a good idea to keep them displayed, and the figures used throughout this book show the sheet tabs turned on.

THE STATUS BAR

At the bottom of the Excel program window is the *status bar*. The status bar is used to display the setting of certain toggle keys, provide quick help, prompt you for some types of input, and display other general status information. The status bar typically looks like this:

If you do not see the status bar on your screen, it has probably been turned off. If you want to check this, select Options from the Tools menu. When you do, you will see the Workspace Options dialog box, shown in Figure 4.5.

View file card

Controls status bar

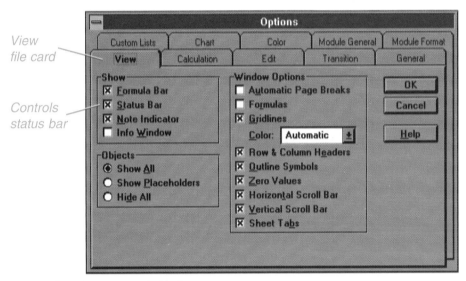

Figure 4.5 The Options dialog box.

If an × appears to the left of the Status Bar option on this dialog box, then the status bar should appear at the bottom of the Excel program window. If the × does not appear, click on the Status Bar option until it does. When you are satisfied with the setting, click on the OK button.

Take a look at the status bar again. The left side of the status bar indicates any messages or help ideas that are pertinent to what you are doing. The rest of the status bar is used to indicate the condition of keys such as NUM LOCK or CAPS LOCK.

WHAT YOU NEED TO KNOW

Excel provides a complete environment in which you can create your documents. In this lesson you have learned about several important facets of that environment. In particular, you have learned that:

- ☑ Toolbars provide a quick, easy way to access common Excel commands. The two most commonly used toolbars are the standard toolbar and the formatting toolbar.

- ☑ You can control which toolbars are displayed by using the Toolbars option from the View menu.

- ☑ The formula bar is used to indicate your position on the sheet as well as the contents of the current cell.

- ☑ Using sheet tabs, you can quickly select which sheet of your workbook you want to use.

- ☑ The status bar, which appears at the bottom of the Excel window, provides you with information about menu choices or the status of keyboard control keys.

A firm understanding of these elements will make your time with Excel much more productive. Before proceeding with the other lessons in this book, make sure you have turned on each of these elements so they are displayed. If you have any questions about how to do this, refer to the detailed instructions earlier in this lesson.

In the next lesson you will learn how to select a sheet from your workbook and how to scroll through a sheet with keyboard and mouse.

Lesson 5

How to Get Around in Excel

It is fairly safe to say that virtually none of the workbooks you create with Excel will fit on one screen. It is not unusual to have workbooks that are quite large, encompassing many rows and columns. In this lesson you will learn how to move through your Excel workbook, as well as how to move around sheets in your workbook. In particular, you will learn how to

- Select a sheet from your workbook

- Use the keyboard to move through a sheet

- Use the mouse to scroll through a sheet

SELECTING A SHEET

In Lesson 4 you learned that you can use the sheet tabs to control which sheet is displayed on the screen. Take another look at the sheet tabs at the bottom of your Excel document window:

Each of the tabs, labeled **Sheet1** through **Sheet6**, represents an individual sheet in your workbook. The tab shown in white is the sheet that is currently displayed. If you want to display a different sheet, simply use the mouse to point to the tab for that sheet and click the left mouse button.

When you first start Excel, a brand new workbook is displayed. Workbooks, when they are new, always contain 16 sheets. In the sheet tab illustration just shown, you can only see tabs for six of those sheets. If you want to see the tabs for the other sheets, use the tools at the left side of the sheet tabs. Table 5.1 shows what each of these tools does.

Button	Function
	Displays the leftmost sheet tabs
	Scrolls the sheet tabs left
	Scrolls the sheet tabs right
	Displays the rightmost sheet tabs

Table 5.1. The sheet tab controls.

Moving Around a Sheet

Once you have selected a sheet on which you want to work, you can move around it using either the keyboard or the mouse. The following sections detail both methods of movement.

Using the Keyboard

Using the keyboard to move around a sheet is very intuitive. If you have used the cursor-control keys in other programs, you will probably feel right at home with the use of the keys in Excel. For instance, you can press PgUp or PgDn to move up or down a screen in your sheet. Likewise, the arrow keys (Left Arrow, Right Arrow, Up Arrow, and Down Arrow) move the cursor one space in the direction indicated by the arrow.

Some movement is performed by using the cursor-control keys in conjunction with other keys. For instance, pressing Ctrl-Home results in moving the cursor to the beginning of the sheet. Table 5.2 describes the movement actions you can perform from the keyboard:

Key	Alone	With Ctrl Key
PgUp	Up one screen	Previous sheet
PgDn	Down one screen	Next sheet
Left Arrow	Left one cell	Next cell to the left containing information
Right Arrow	Right one cell	Next cell to the right containing information
Up Arrow	Up one cell	Next cell up containing information
Down Arrow	Down one cell	Next cell down containing information

Table 5.2 Cursor-movement keystrokes.

Don't be put off by the size of this list. Instead, focus on the few keystrokes you will use to do most of your movement. Other keypresses can be learned as needed.

Notice from Table 5.2 that the Home and End keys are not listed. This is because their behavior differs, based on how you use them. For instance, pressing Home will typically select the cell at the beginning of the row, and Ctrl-Home moves you to the beginning of the sheet. If you have the Scroll Lock key turned on, Home functions differently. In this case, both Home and Ctrl-Home move to the first cell on the current screen.

The END key is a special case. If you press END, nothing happens. This is because Excel expects you to use END with another key. For instance, if you press END-RIGHT ARROW, you move to the cell preceding the first empty cell to the right of your current location. If there is nothing but empty cells, you are moved to the last possible cell on the row (column IV). The UP ARROW, DOWN ARROW, LEFT ARROW, and RIGHT ARROW keys all function similarly when used with END. While this might sound confusing, it all becomes very clear if you try it out.

CTRL-END moves you to the last cell containing information in the lower-right corner of your sheet. If you use END with the SCROLL LOCK key turned on, it simply selects the bottom-right cell on the current screen.

In future lessons you will learn how you can enter information in your workbook. As you do so, you will notice that the cursor-control keys function differently when you are editing the contents of a cell. In this instance, they do not necessarily result in moving to different cells; they move the editing cursor through the characters in the cell itself. You will learn more about how this works in Lesson 6 and Lesson 7.

USING THE MOUSE

To use the mouse to move the cursor, simply point to the desired cell on the sheet and click the left mouse button. Clearly, this can only work if the cell you want is visible on the screen. If it is not visible, you will need to *scroll* (think of a rolled-up scroll of paper) through your sheet until the desired cell is visible. Scrolling is accomplished by using the *scroll bars* on the screen, shown in Figure 5.1:

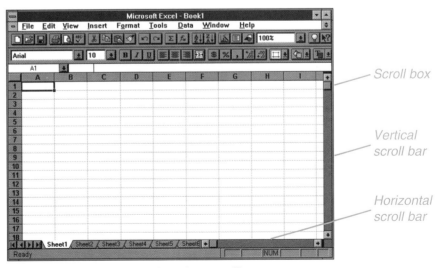

Scroll box

Vertical scroll bar

Horizontal scroll bar

Figure 5.1 *Use scroll bars to view parts of the sheet that are off screen.*

Consider each scroll bar as a rather fluid representation of the size of your sheet in the indicated direction. Thus, the bottom of the vertical scroll bar represents the bottom of your sheet. The small square within the scroll bar, the *scroll box,* represents where the portion of the sheet displayed on your screen falls within your sheet, from beginning to end. Thus, if the scroll box is halfway between the top and bottom of the vertical scroll bar, then what you see on your screen is halfway through your sheet. The horizontal scroll bar works in much the same way, except it represents your sheet horizontally (left to right), rather than vertically.

Using the scroll bars is easy; there are several ways you can use them to scroll through your sheet. Perhaps the easiest method is to use the mouse to point your cursor at one of the arrows at the end of the scroll bars and click the arrow with the mouse. When you do, the sheet is scrolled in that direction, a row (vertically) or a column (horizontally) at a time. Another way to use the scroll bars is to use the mouse to click above or below the block in the scroll bar, as shown in Figure 5.2:

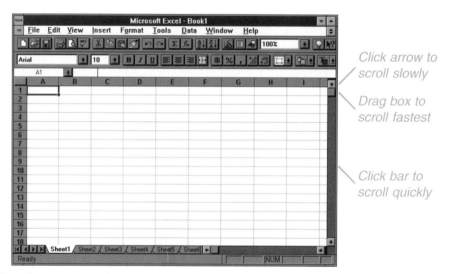

Figure 5.2 Scrolling features in Excel.

When you do, the sheet is scrolled one *screen* at a time in the indicated direction. Finally, you can move large distances by using the mouse to drag the scroll box within the scroll bar. For instance, if you wanted to scroll to the middle of your sheet, simply point to the scroll box, click and hold down the left mouse button, and then move the mouse. As you do, the scroll box moves as well. When you release the mouse button, the sheet window is adjusted to display the cells at the relative position indicated by the block.

Note: *When you use the scroll bars to move through your sheet, the selected cell does not actually change. Instead, you are only changing what you view on your screen. If you want to select a different cell, you must still point somewhere on your screen and click with the mouse.*

WHAT YOU NEED TO KNOW

Before you can begin working effectively in Excel, you must know how to move around your workbook and sheets. The features presented in this lesson allow you to both move the cursor and scroll the sheet in many different ways. You have learned how to

☑ The sheet tabs allow you to control which sheet you use. The buttons to the left of the sheet tabs control which sheet tabs you see.

☑ You can use the cursor-control keys to move around your sheet, much as you use them in a word processor.

☑ Using the mouse to click on the scroll bar results in different parts of the sheet being displayed.

If you are a bit hazy about how to do any of these tasks, take a minute to review the lesson and find the necessary steps.

In the next lesson you will learn how to enter information into a sheet; how to select a cell or group of cells; and how to change, move, or copy information.

Section Two

CREATING WORKBOOKS

Workbooks are to Excel what documents are to a word processor. They contain the numbers, text, and formulas that combine to present your information clearly. In this section you will learn how to use workbooks—how to enter and change information, how to work with formulas, what names are and how they are used, and how you can benefit from array formulas. You will also learn how to save, load, and print your workbook. Each of these are skills that you will use time and again in Excel. By the time you complete this section, you will be able to enter and edit information using the full capabilities of the program.

Lesson 6

Entering and Changing Information

The most fundamental purpose of any spreadsheet program is to allow you to enter information, define relationships, and create output either as a report, a chart, or a combination of the two. In this respect, Excel is no different than any other spreadsheet program. In addition, however, Excel has many powerful tools that allow you to perform other types of actions in regard to your data. In this lesson you will learn how Excel enables you to accomplish two of the three fundamental purposes. This lesson covers

- How to enter information

- How to edit what you type

- How to select ranges of cells

- How to move or copy information

ENTERING YOUR INFORMATION

When you first start Excel, you will probably see a workbook already open and ready for you to enter information, as shown in Figure 6.1.

It is possible, however, that your version of Excel doesn't start with an empty workbook on the screen. If this is the case, simply click on the ⬛ tool on the toolbar. This creates a new workbook, ready for you to use. Notice the title bar at the top of the document window (the window containing the workbook), or, if your document window is maximized, the title bar at the top of the Excel program window. It indicates a sheet name, such as Book1, Book2, Book3, or so on. This lets you know you are working with a brand new workbook—one that has not been given a name yet.

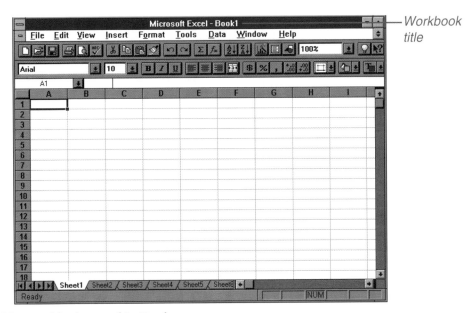

Figure 6.1 *New workbook opened in Excel.*

When you have a blank workbook open, you are ready to begin entering information. All you need to do is to select the cell in which you want to enter information and then start typing. If you select a cell that already contains information, the new information you type will replace the old information. As you type, Excel displays your information in two places on the screen—in the cell you selected and in the formula bar, as you can see in Figure 6.2.

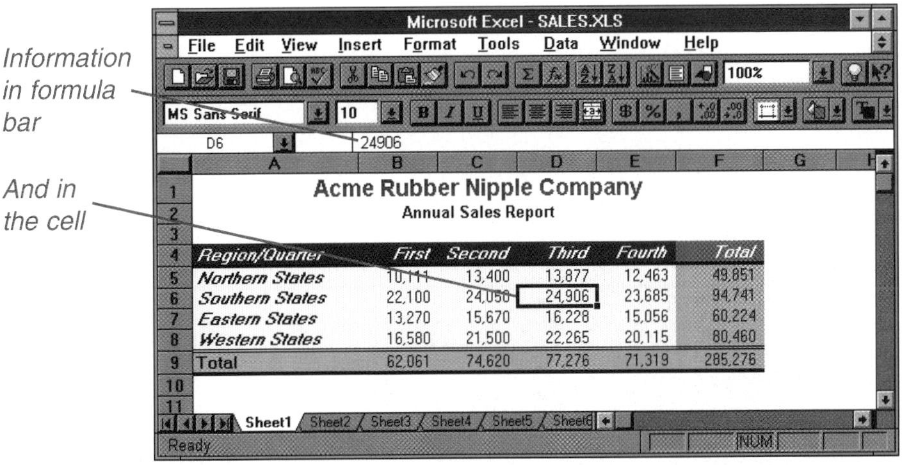

Figure 6.2 *Information being entered in Excel.*

There are four types of information you can enter in a cell. You can enter text (nothing but letters and numbers), numbers (with no letters), dates, or formulas. If you are entering text, numbers, or dates, all the information you type appears in the cell until you press ENTER or press one of the cursor-control keys (introduced in Lesson 5). If you are entering formulas (covered in Lesson 7), you need to press ENTER to signify that you have finished working in a cell.

As you select different cells within the sheet, notice that the contents of the cell are displayed in the formula bar at the top of the program window. Excel also makes an attempt to format the information that is displayed within the workbook. This means that there might not be enough room to display the information within the cell, as shown in Figure 6.3.

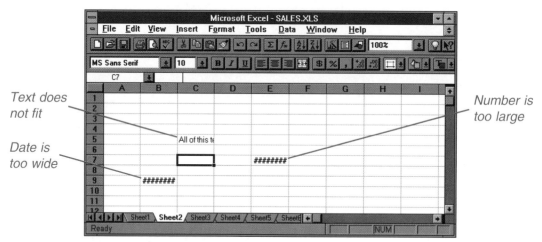

Figure 6.3 *Formatting problems in Excel.*

If you find yourself in this situation, you will need to either change the contents of the cell, change the formatting applied by Excel, or change the width of the column of cells. Changing the contents of a cell is covered in the rest of this lesson, while changing the formatting is covered in Section 3. Changing the column width is covered in Lesson 16.

CHANGING THE INFORMATION YOU ENTER

There will come a time when you want to change what you have entered in a cell. This changing process is referred to as *editing.* Editing requires that you first select the cell whose contents you want to edit. Once this is done, you can edit information in a cell in one of two ways. The first is to move the mouse pointer into the cell information displayed on the formula bar, and then click the left mouse button, as shown here:

Click anywhere on this information to edit it

When you do this, you can make any changes you like to the information. The cursor-control keys then function as they would in a word processor, as shown in Table 6.1.

Key	Alone	With CTRL Key
HOME	Start of line	Start of cell
END	End of line	End of cell
LEFT ARROW	Left one character	Left one word
RIGHT ARROW	Right one character	Right one word
UP ARROW	Up one line	Up one line
DOWN ARROW	Down one line	Down one line

Table 6.1 Cursor-movement keystrokes when editing a cell.

All the keys you press (letters, numbers, and so on) are considered to be changes to the cell you are editing. When you are through editing, press ENTER.

The other way to edit information in a cell is to select the cell and press the F2 key. This is functionally equivalent to using the mouse to edit cell contents, as just described, except that the full cell contents appear within the body of your sheet, where you can edit them directly. An example might look like this:

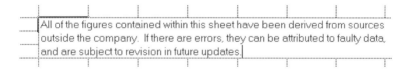

Note: *Rather than pressing* **F2**, *you can edit information within a cell by using the mouse to point to the cell and then double-clicking the mouse button.*

When editing cell contents in this fashion, all keys function the same as previously described in Table 6.1.

SELECTING INFORMATION IN A CELL

If a cell contains a great deal of information, you might want to use some advanced editing techniques to change that information. In general, edits within a cell are done by selecting what you want to change and then choosing the function that makes the change. In order to change information, you must first *select* it. Selected information is *highlighted*—light against a dark background, as opposed to the normal dark against a light background. Selecting information is done by *extending* the cursor; extending the cursor is done in one of three ways: using the SHIFT key and the cursor-control keys, the **F8** key, or the mouse.

SELECTING INFORMATION WITH THE SHIFT KEY

With your cursor located at one end of the information you want to select, press and hold down the SHIFT key. As you hold it down, continue to use the cursor-control keys. Notice that the cursor highlighting expands to include more and more information as you move it. For instance, the words *can be attributed* are selected in the following:

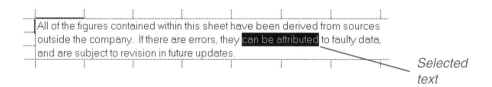

All of the figures contained within this sheet have been derived from sources outside the company. If there are errors, they can be attributed to faulty data, and are subject to revision in future updates.

Selected text

SELECTING INFORMATION WITH THE F8 KEY

If you don't want to hold down the SHIFT key, you can also use the **F8** key to mark the beginning of a selection. When you do this, **EXT** (meaning *extension*) appears on the status bar, like this:

Indicates extension
mode is on

As you then move the cursor, the selection is extended to include everything between where you pressed **F8** and the current cursor position. To turn off extension mode, simply press an editing key or press Esc.

SELECTING INFORMATION WITH THE MOUSE

If you prefer, you can use the mouse to make selections. This is done by dragging the mouse across the information you want to select. Move the mouse cursor so it is positioned at one end of what you want to select. Then press and hold down the left mouse button. As you move the mouse (with the button held down), the selection grows. To end the selection, release the mouse button. You can also use the mouse to select a whole word by simply double-clicking on the word. If you double-click a word and then, while still holding the mouse button down, drag (forward or backward) across more text, the information will be selected one word at a time, rather than one letter at a time, which can be handy.

QUICK REVIEW

Excel allows you to select information within a cell quickly and easily. This is done by any of the following methods:

1. Holding down the SHIFT key and using the cursor-control keys.

2. Pressing F8 key to toggle select mode on and off, and then using the cursor-control keys.

3. Holding down the left mouse button and moving the mouse to select the desired information.

SELECTING CELLS

Sometimes, you might want to edit the contents of more than a single cell. This is done by selecting the cells you want affected. There are several ways you can select cells, as detailed in the following sections.

Selecting a Row or Column

Selecting entire rows or columns in a sheet is extremely easy. It is done most easily with the mouse. To select rows or columns, click in the border areas shown in Figure 6.4. When you do, the entire row, column, or sheet is highlighted, signifying it has been selected.

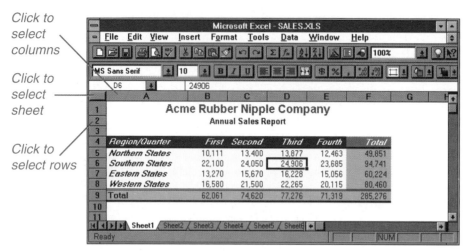

Click to select columns

Click to select sheet

Click to select rows

Figure 6.4 Selecting a row, column, or sheet.

Selecting a Block of Cells

A *block* of cells is nothing but a rectangular area within a sheet. Figure 6.5 illustrates what a block of cells looks like, once they are selected.

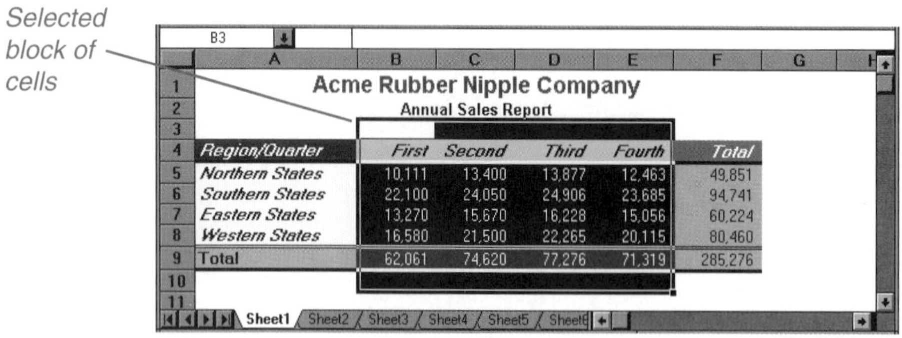

Selected block of cells

Figure 6.5 A block of cells.

To select a block of cells, you use the same techniques used to select information within a single cell. The first step is to select the cell at one corner of the block. In Figure 6.5, this is cell B3. Then, extend the selection using either the SHIFT key, the **F8** key, or the mouse, as detailed earlier in this lesson.

SELECTING A GROUP OF CELLS

A *group* of cells, as opposed to a block, is any collection of cells that is not rectangular in nature. For example, Figure 6.6 shows an example of a group of cells, each of which is highlighted (selected).

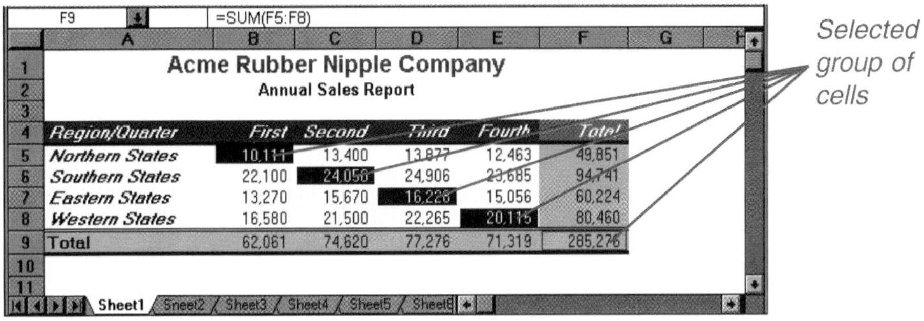

Figure 6.6 A group of cells.

To select a group of cells, simply point to the first cell in the group with the mouse pointer and then click on the left mouse button. This selects the first cell. Then, hold down the CTRL key as you continue to select other cells within the group. Each cell you click on (while you hold down the CTRL key) is highlighted as it is added to the group.

QUICK REVIEW

Excel allows you to select cells quickly and easily. This is done by any of the following methods:

- Selecting a row or column is done by clicking in the row or column header.

- Selecting a contiguous range of cells is done by pointing to a corner of the range, clicking and holding the left mouse button, and dragging the mouse to the opposite corner of the range.

- Selecting a non-contiguous group of cells is done by holding down the CTRL key as you select (with the mouse) each cell or range of cells you want added to the group.

MAKING LARGER EDITS

Once you have selected any number of cells (or a block of information within a cell), you can edit it in a number of ways. For instance, if you press either BACKSPACE or DEL, the selection is deleted—DEL empties the whole group, but BACKSPACE clears only the last cell selected in the group. You can accomplish much the same task, on a cell or *contiguous* (solid, with no gaps) rows or columns, by pressing CTRL-X. The difference is that CTRL-X saves the selection to the *Clipboard*, a memory location from which you can then paste it into a new spot, whereas DEL and BACKSPACE do not. Pressing CTRL-X is referred to as *cutting* information, while pressing DEL or BACKSPACE is referred to as *clearing* information. The significance of being able to cut information, as opposed to clearing it, will become apparent in the next section.

One other feature of Excel is that when you have made a selection and you start typing without first deleting the highlighted information, the information you type *replaces* the selection you have made. This is very powerful, removing the need to clear existing information explicitly before you being typing again.

MOVING AND COPYING INFORMATION

Two common editing tasks are moving information around in your sheet and copying existing information to a different location in your sheet. Both of these functions are very closely related to each other. They are accomplished by first selecting the information you want to move or copy, as described earlier in this lesson. You can move or copy either information within a cell, entire rows or columns, or blocks of cells. You cannot move or copy groups of cells (those that are not a rectangular block).

Once the information to be moved or copied is selected, you can move it by using the Clipboard. Earlier you learned that you can use CTRL-X to cut information from your sheet. This is the cutting part of the process called *cutting and pasting,* which is the same as moving information. Once it has been cut, you need only position the cursor where you want the information moved or select the cell where you want a range of cells copied, and press CTRL-V to *paste* (insert) the information at that location.

If you want to copy the information, the process is the same, except that you press CTRL-C instead of CTRL-X. This command copies the selection to the Clipboard, leaving the original. You can then move the cursor or select another cell and paste the selection wherever you desire.

If you ever forget these commands (CTRL-V, CTRL-C, and CTRL-X), they are also available as menu choices from the Edit menu, a portion of which is shown here:

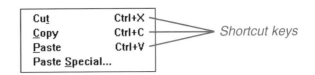

Note that the shortcut keys that are available for an action are shown to the right of that action on the menu. If you want more information about copying the contents of cells, refer to Lesson 8, "Copying, Moving, and Deleting Information."

WHAT YOU NEED TO KNOW

Entering and editing information is the basis of everything you do in Excel. In this lesson you have learned the ground rules that Excel uses in allowing you to enter and edit information within a sheet. In particular, you have learned the following:

☑ Entering information in a cell is as easy as selecting the cell and starting to type.

☑ Information within a cell can be changed by using many of the same techniques used to edit other information, such as word processing documents.

☑ To edit larger parts of a sheet, you can use the mouse to select entire rows, columns, and groups of cells.

☑ You can move the contents of cells by selecting them and then cutting them using CTRL-X. Select where you want the cells moved, and then paste them using CTRL-V.

☑ To copy the contents of cells you first select them and press CTRL-C. You can then select where you want them copied and press CTRL-V to actually paste them.

As you continue to use Excel, these skills will become second nature. Before you know it, you will find it just as easy to change information as it is to enter it in the first place.

In the next lesson you will learn about entering and editing formulas.

Lesson 7

Entering and Changing Formulas

In Lesson 6 you learned how you can enter and edit information in an Excel workbook. While entering numbers and text may work for many spreadsheet uses, the real power lies in the ability to define relationships between cells. These relationships are defined by the use of *formulas*. In this lesson you will learn the basics of entering formulas; specifically, you will discover the following:

- What a formula is
- How to enter a formula
- Using functions in your formulas
- Making changes to a formula

WHAT IS A FORMULA?

In Excel, a formula is very close to what you learned from your elementary school math teacher. For instance, the following are all examples of formulas:

$$2 + 2 = 4$$

$$18 \div 3 = 6$$

$$A - B = C$$

Each of these is probably very familiar to you. However, in Excel, you use formulas to define what the contents of a cell should be. Since the information referred to by the formula can change (it might be the contents of other cells), the formulas in Excel most closely resemble the third example just provided.

HOW TO ENTER A FORMULA

Entering a formula in Excel is simple. All you need to do is start it with the equal sign, and then provide the formula parts. The equal sign tells Excel that what follows is a formula, and not merely a label or bit of text. For instance, let's suppose you have two cells defined in your sheet. Cell A1 contains the number 7, and cell A2 contains the number 5. Now suppose that you want cell A3 to be equal to the difference between the other two cells. To do this, you select a cell, A3 for example, and enter the following formula:

=A1–A2

When you press ENTER, Excel replaces the formula with the result of the formula, in this case, it would be the number 2 (7 minus 5 is 2). This result is shown in Figure 7.1:

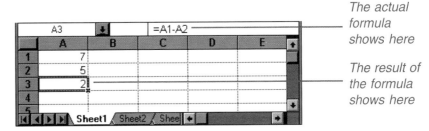

Figure 7.1 The formula is replaced with its result.

You have just entered your first formula. In cell A3 you defined a relationship between that cell and others in the sheet. The beauty of Excel is that if you change the contents of either cell A1 or A2, then the value displayed in A3 is recalculated. For instance, if you change A1 so it contains the number 49, your screen will appear as shown in Figure 7.2:

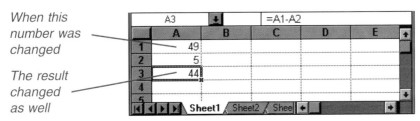

Figure 7.2 The formula is recalculated when another cell is changed.

TYPES OF OPERATORS

To make formulas meaningful, Excel lets you use *operators*. These are nothing more than symbols that define the relationship between two or more cell references. Take another look at the following formula:

$$= A1 - A2$$

Cell references

Operator

49

In this case, the minus sign is the operator. This is not the only operator that Excel supports, however. There are several types of operators that are supported by Excel. The most common type, arithmetic operators, are listed in Table 7.1.

Operator	Meaning
+	Addition
–	Subtraction
*	Multiplication
/	Division
%	Percent (placcd after a value)
^	Exponent (as in 8^3, which is 8 raised to the 3rd power)

Table 7.1 The arithmetic operators.

Excel also supports Boolean, or comparison, operators. These operators are used to compare two values or expressions, returning either the logical value TRUE or the value FALSE. (These are special values supported by Excel to represent the outcome of a comparison.) The comparison operators are listed in Table 7.2.

Operator	Meaning
=	Equal to
>	Greater than
>=	Greater than or equal to
<	Less than
<=	Less than or equal to
<>	Not equal to

Table 7.2 The comparison operators.

Finally, Excel also provides a text operator, which is used to combine (or *concatenate*) text. This operator is the ampersand (&).

How Operators Are Evaluated

The operators in a formula are generally evaluated from left to right. Thus, in the following formula the addition is performed first and then the subtraction:

$$= C7 + A2 - B3 \quad\text{———— Operations evaluated left to right}$$

However, this is not always the case. For instance, Excel will perform any exponentiation first, then multiplication or division, then addition or subtraction, then text concatenation, and finally any comparisons. Thus, in the following formula, the multiplication is performed before the addition, even though the multiplication occurs to the right of the addition:

= C12 + D4 * A1 ——————— *Multiplication performed first*

If you want to change the order in which the operations are performed, you can use parentheses. For instance, if you wanted the addition to occur before the multiplication in the previous formula, you would enter it like this:

= (C12 + D4) * A1 ——————— *Operation in parentheses performed first*

CELL REFERENCES

You have probably noticed that references to other cells are the heart of any Excel formula. While it is possible to construct a formula using only numbers, it is more meaningful to use these references to other cells.

There are two types of references in Excel—relative references and absolute references. *Relative references* are called that because they are relative to the cell in which the formula is contained. All the formulas used in this lesson so far use relative references. They use references such as A1, B7, and C12.

Absolute references, on the other hand, are not relative to the cell in which the formula is contained. Instead, they provide an absolute, unchanging reference to a specific cell. These use a dollar sign before the row and column designators. Thus, examples of absolute references would be A1, B7, and C12.

Excel also lets you mix relative and absolute references. This means you can make either the row or column reference absolute and the other relative. For instance, the reference $A1 means that the column reference is absolute, but the row reference is not. Conversely, in the reference B$7, the column reference is relative and the row reference is absolute.

How you use references in your formulas—relative, absolute, or mixed—is up to you. The real significance of these different types of references will become apparent in Lesson 8 and the rest of the book.

USING FUNCTIONS IN FORMULAS

So far you have learned how you can use numbers and cell references in your formulas. You have seen how operators are used to glue a formula together. But what if you wanted to use a square root in your formula, or you needed to create a sum of a range of figures? Excel recognizes the need to do this, and provides predefined *functions*, which can be used to perform a variety of purposes in a formula. For instance, take a look at the following formula:

= AVERAGE(C2:C7)

This formula uses the AVERAGE function to return the statistical average of the values in the six cells from C2 to C7. Notice that the function uses *arguments,* enclosed within the parentheses, as a basis for completing its tasks. This example also introduces another important concept—references to cell *ranges.* A range of cells can be used by simply defining the boundaries (C2 and C7) and separating them with a colon. Excel understands this as "everything between C7 and C7, inclusive." The alternative to using ranges would be to enter the formula in the following manner:

= AVERAGE(C2 + C3 + C4 + C5 + C6 + C7)

For small ranges, this might be acceptable, but if you are dealing with a large range, this quickly becomes tiresome and cumbersome. It is much better to define a range with a colon.

Not every function uses ranges as arguments. For instance, the following formula uses the square root of 2:

Function

= E17 * SQRT(2)

Argument

There are also functions that don't require any arguments at all, as in the following:

$$= PI() * F4\wedge2$$

Function ——————— (pointing to PI)

No argument ——————— (pointing to ())

This is the formula to find the area of a circle, assuming that the value in F4 is the radius of the circle.

Excel provides over 200 such functions, divided into nine different categories. These categories include the following:

- Statistical functions
- Date and time functions
- Mathematical and trigonometric functions
- Financial functions
- Lookup and reference functions
- Database functions
- Logical functions
- Text functions
- Information functions

Excel also supports user-defined functions, but those are beyond the scope of this book. If you want more information on the available functions, refer to the online Help system (Lesson 2) which lists the available functions and gives a short description of what they do.

FUNCTION SHORTCUTS

While it is possible to type a function directly into a formula, this can be a little overwhelming. Particularly with over 200 functions to choose from, each with their own arguments and nuances. Recognizing that functions can sometimes be overwhelming, Excel provides two tools, on the standard toolbar, which you can use for help with functions. The first, and simplest of the tools is the summation tool (Σ). This tool is designed to be used when you want to quickly insert a formula to sum up a row or column. For instance, let's suppose your sheet looks similar to that shown in Figure 7.3:

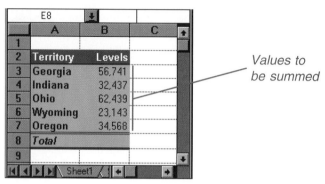

Figure 7.3 A list of numbers to be summed.

To perform a summation, all you need to do is select cell B8 (where you want the totals to be), and then click on the ∑ tool. Excel then inserts the following formula in the cell, as if you had typed it:

=SUM(B3:B7)

This is the range that Excel determined you wanted to sum. All you need to do is press ENTER, and the formula is complete. Your finished sheet looks like the one in Figure 7.4:

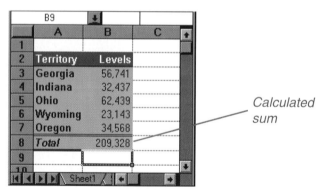

Figure 7.4 The sum of the numbers is calculated and displayed.

The other shortcut is the Function Wizard. This is a tool that assists you in properly inserting a function into a formula. All you need to do is type your formula until you are ready to insert a function. Then either choose Function from the Insert menu, or click on the *fx* tool on the standard toolbar. When you do, you will see the dialog box shown in Figure 7.5:

Choose a
function
category

Choose the
function name

A description
of the selected
function

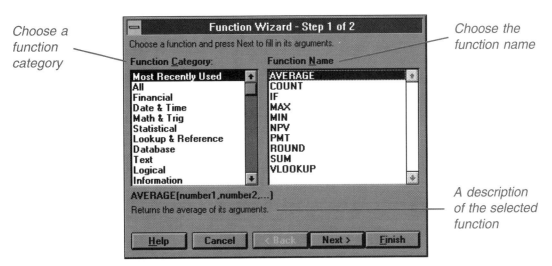

Figure 7.5 The first step of the Function Wizard.

Choose the function category (discussed earlier) and the function name you want to use. Then click on the Next > button. You will then see the second part of the dialog box, which is shown in Figure 7.6:

Figure 7.6 The second step of the Function Wizard.

The second step in using the Function Wizard involves providing the arguments that are to be used by the function. Exactly how this dialog box appears depends on the function you are inserting in your formula. All you need to do is provide the appropriate arguments and then click on the Finish button. The function is inserted into your formula.

MAKING CHANGES TO A FORMULA

Changing a formula is just as easy as changing any other cell information in Excel. If you want to change it, you first select the cell in which the formula resides and use one of the editing techniques described in Lesson 6.

When you are making changes to a formula, there are two easy mistakes you can make. The first is to change cell references without realizing it. Make sure you don't delete a number or letter that messes up a cell reference. The other common mistake is to delete a parentheses used in the formula. As you already know, parentheses, are used to specify which parts of the formula are performed first, and they are used to denote arguments for functions. Make sure that your formulas have the same number of left and right parentheses, and that they are in the right places.

WHAT YOU NEED TO KNOW

Formulas are where Excel really shines. In this lesson you have learned about formulas and had a quick introduction to functions. In particular, you have learned the following:

- ☑ Formulas are used to derive values based on relationships between other cells in your workbook.

- ☑ Formulas are entered by first using the equal sign and then entering cell references along with an operator.

- ☑ Excel provides many different operators which can be used to define relationships between cells.

- ☑ Cell references are entered in a formula using the coordinates of the cell, such as A2. Cell ranges are entered by putting a colon between two cells references that define the range, such as A2:B7.

- ☑ Functions are used to perform more complex operations in a formula. Excel provides over 200 functions you can use to add power and flexibility to your formulas.

- ☑ Functions are most easily entered by using the FunctionWizard from the standard toolbar.

If you are unclear on any of these topics, it is important that you review and work with them until you understand them fully. Both formulas and functions are critical to your effective use of Excel.

In the next lesson you will learn how to cut, copy, clear, delete, and duplicate cells.

Lesson 8

Copying, Moving, and Deleting Information

So far in this section you have learned how to enter information in an Excel workbook and how to enter formulas. In Lesson 6 you learned a bit about how to move and copy information. This lesson deals more specifically with how you move cell contents from one place to another and otherwise manipulate them. You will learn how to

- Copy cells
- Cut cells
- Clear cells
- Delete cells
- Duplicate cells

As you learn each of these skills, you will also learn what happens to the cell references that might be in the cells you are copying, moving, or deleting.

HOW TO COPY CELLS

In Lesson 6 you learned, in general, how to copy information from one place to another. The same general guidelines are applicable whether you are editing the contents of a single cell, or copying entire cells. Basically, you do the following:

1. Decide which cells you want to copy and then select them.

2. Choose the Copy command from the Edit menu, press CTRL-C, or select the ▣ tool from the standard toolbar. (Old-time Excel users also know you can also press CTRL-INSERT, if desired.)

3. Select the cell where you want to copy the original selection.

4. Choose the Paste command from the Edit menu, press CTRL-V, select the ▣ tool from the standard toolbar, or simply press ENTER.

5. If you did not press ENTER in step 4, you can repeat steps 3 and 4 until you have copied the selection as many times as desired.

As an example of how to copy cells, let's assume you started with the sheet shown in Figure 8.1. You wanted to duplicate the range of cells at A4:F9, and place them at A12:F17.

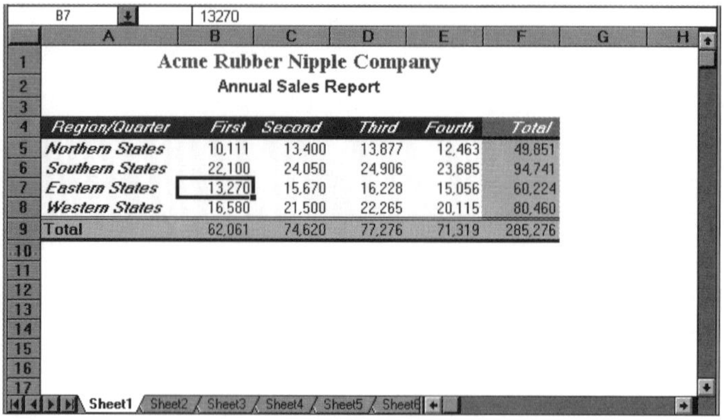

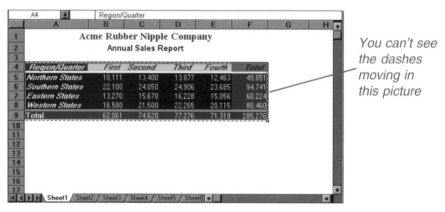

Figure 8.1 The original sheet.

The first step is to select the cells you want to copy. The easiest way is to select them with the mouse, as described in Lesson 6. Then press CTRL-C, and a moving, dashed line appears around the selection. This is shown in Figure 8.2. (Obviously, the "moving" part is not shown; you'll either have to try it yourself or take my word for it.)

Figure 8.2 After using the Copy command.

At this point, the selection has been copied to the Clipboard and can be pasted elsewhere on this sheet or on any other sheet. Since you only want to make a copy of this information in the range

A12:F17, you should select the cell at A12. This marks the upper-left corner of where you want the selection pasted. There is no need to select a range of cells as large as the original selection, although you can if you desire. If, instead, you select a single cell, then Excel assumes that you want the copy of the original selection to begin at that location.

Now press ENTER. The information is pasted at the new location, as shown in Figure 8.3.

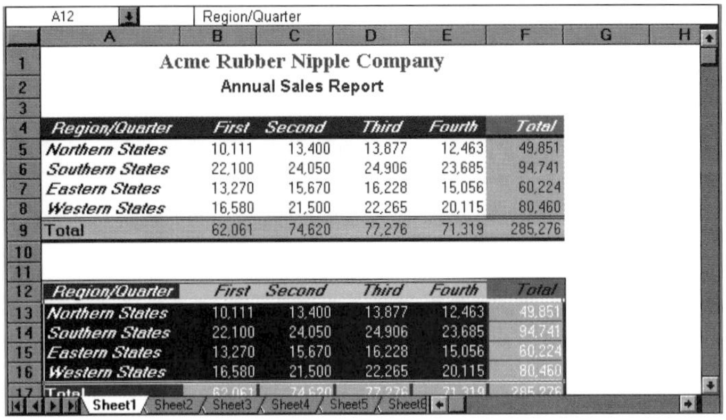

Figure 8.3 After pasting the selection.

If you scroll down a bit, you will notice something interesting about the newly pasted cells. They look exactly like the original! While this might not seem surprising at first glance, notice that the cells that contain formulas (in the totals row and column) are also correct. This is because Excel translated the cell references in the original selection into the correct cell references in the pasted cells. For instance, if you were to look at the original total for the Northern States region, at cell F5, you will notice that it contains the following formula:

        =SUM(B5:E5)

If you take a look at the corresponding cell in the pasted area, cell F13, you will notice that it contains the following formula:

        =SUM(B13:E13)

This is because Excel has translated the relative references in the original formula to the correct references in the resulting formula. Had the original references been absolute—that is, they were preceded by a dollar sign ($)—then Excel would not have done any translation, and there would have been no difference between the two formulas.

How to Cut Cells

Cutting cells means that you remove them from one place in your sheet and paste them at another. In effect, cutting (in Excel) is the same as moving (in other applications). This is easily done by following these steps:

1. Decide which cells you want to cut, and then select them.

2. Choose the Cut command from the Edit menu, press CTRL-X, or select the ✂ tool from the standard toolbar.

3. Select the cell where you want to paste what you are cutting.

4. Choose the Paste command from the Edit menu, press CTRL-V, select the 📋 tool from the standard toolbar, or simply press ENTER.

As an example of cutting, let's assume you want to begin with the same spreadsheet that you ended up with at the beginning of the previous section (see Figure 8.3). This time, you want to cut the fourth-quarter figures. To do this, select the cells at E13:E16, and then press CTRL-X. The same moving, dotted line appears around the selection that was described in the previous section.

Next, select the cell where you want the information pasted. For the purposes of this example, choose the cell at E20, and press ENTER. The selection is cut and pasted at the new location, as shown in Figure 8.4.

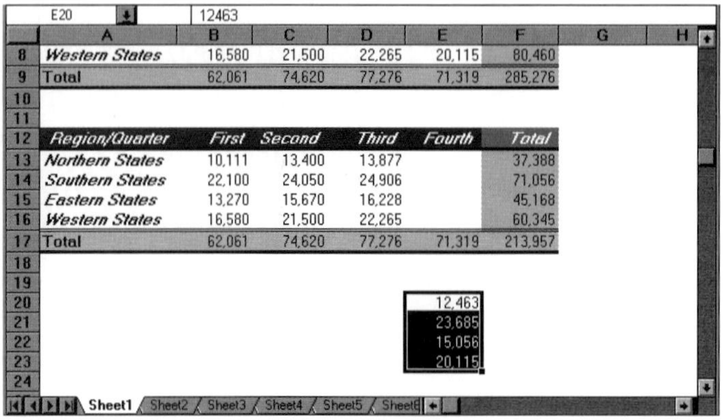

Figure 8.4 After cutting and pasting the selection.

You might be wondering how cutting and pasting this selection affected the formulas that depended on the selection that was cut—good question. There are five cells containing formulas that were directly dependent upon the values in the cut selection. Table 8.1 details these cells and their formulas before and after the cut and paste.

Cell	Before Cut	After Paste
F13	=SUM(B13:E13)	same
F14	=SUM(B14:E14)	same
F15	=SUM(B15:E15)	same
F16	=SUM(B16:E16)	same
E17	=SUM(E13:E16)	=SUM(E20:E23)

Table 8.1 *Effects of a cut-and-paste operation.*

Notice that only one formula changed. This is because it was the only formula entirely dependent on the selection that was cut and pasted. Excel could make a change, so it did. The other formulas did not change, since they only relied upon a portion of the selection being cut and pasted.

The result of this is that the total at E17 did not change, since it followed the moved range of cells. The results at the other locations did change, however (see Figure 8.4), because part of the information they relied upon for their original totals is no longer there.

As with the copying process described earlier, if you use absolute references in your formulas, then Excel will not modify them at all.

QUICK REVIEW

In Excel, cutting and copying are very similar. The only difference between the two operations is that cutting removes the original information from your sheet, while copying does not. Both operations place information in the Clipboard, where it can later be pasted to a new location.

To cut information, select what you want to cut and press CTRL-X, click on [✂], or choose Cut from the Edit menu.

To copy information, select what you want to copy and press CTRL-C, click on [⧉], or choose Copy from the Edit menu.

To paste information, select the cell or cell range where you want it pasted and press CTRL-V, click on [⧉], or choose Paste from the Edit menu.

How to Clear Cells

Clearing cells is closely akin to cutting them, except you don't need to paste them anywhere else (you can't). Excel lets you clear everything in a cell, or you can clear only the contents, the format, or the notes attached to the cell. (Formatting is covered in Section 3; notes are beyond the scope of this book.) To clear a cell, follow these steps:

1. Decide which cells you want to cut, and then select them.

2. Choose the Clear command from the Edit menu. You will then see a submenu offering you choices of what you can clear:

3. Choose the type of clear you want to perform.

As an alternative, you can simply select a cell and press the DELETE key. This is the same as choosing to delete the contents of a cell. Clearing a cell does not affect any formulas that reference that cell.

How to Delete Cells

Deleting cells is more permanent than virtually any other operation described in this lesson. When you delete a cell, you remove it entirely from your sheet. Don't confuse the cell contents with the cell itself. If you only want to delete the contents, this is called clearing, and was described in the previous section. *Deleting* a cell results in the deletion of the cell and the closing up of the surrounding cells.

To delete a cell, you perform these steps:

1. Decide which cells you want to delete, and then select them.

2. Choose the Delete command from the Edit menu. You will then see the Delete dialog box, as shown in Figure 8.5.

3. Specify how you want Excel to close up the hole the deletion will create.

4. Click on OK

The cells will then be deleted and the surrounding cells moved as you specified.

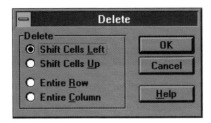

Figure 8.5 The Delete dialog box.

You should note that if you select an entire row or column before choosing the Delete command, you will not see the Delete dialog box shown in Figure 8.6. In this instance, there are no individual cells to move, so Excel doesn't ask.

Perhaps an example of deletion is in order here. Let's assume that you are starting with the sheet shown earlier in Figure 8.3. Further, let's assume that you want to delete the fourth-quarter portion of the second copy of the cells. To do this, you must first select those cells. Use the mouse to select the range E12:E17.

Next, choose Delete from the Edit menu. You will then see the Delete dialog box, previously shown. Make sure that the Shift Cells Left option is selected and then click on OK. The cells are deleted and the ones to the right of it are moved left. The result is shown in Figure 8.6.

	E12	Total					
	A	B	C	D	E	F	G	H
2		Annual Sales Report					
3							
4	*Region/Quarter*	*First*	*Second*	*Third*	*Fourth*	*Total*	
5	*Northern States*	10,111	13,400	13,877	12,463	49,851	
6	*Southern States*	22,100	24,050	24,906	23,685	94,741	
7	*Eastern States*	13,270	15,670	16,228	15,056	60,224	
8	*Western States*	16,580	21,500	22,265	20,115	80,460	
9	Total	62,061	74,620	77,276	71,319	285,276	
10							
11							
12	*Region/Quarter*	*First*	*Second*	*Third*	*Total*		
13	*Northern States*	10,111	13,400	13,877	37,388		
14	*Southern States*	22,100	24,050	24,906	71,056		
15	*Eastern States*	13,270	15,670	16,228	45,168		
16	*Western States*	16,580	21,500	22,265	60,345		
17	Total	62,061	74,620	77,276	213,957		
18							

Sheet1 / Sheet2 / Sheet3 / Sheet4 / Sheet5 / Sheet8

Figure 8.6 The sheet after deleting some cells.

If the sheet contained formulas that referenced the deleted cells, the condition of those formulas after the deletion depends on the type of reference being made. Suppose, for a moment, that E15 was one of the cells being deleted. If a formula contains an explicit reference to E15, then Excel replaces the reference with a reference error. For instance, the following formula:

=E15 * 1.25 + F15

is changed to this after E15 is deleted:

=#REF! * 1.25 + F15

You can then go back and make any changes necessary to correct the formula. If the cell being deleted was part of a range reference in a formula, then Excel can compensate. For instance, suppose that a different formula contained the following:

=SUM(E8:E19)

This is the type of formula that would be in a cell below where E15 was located (perhaps at cell E20). When E15 is deleted, this formula is not changed; the range remains the same. The new value moved into E15 by deleting the original E15 will obviously affect the result of this formula, however. If the formula is to the right of the deleted cell, as in the following:

=SUM(C15:E15)

then Excel will adjust the range for the deleted cell, and the result will be

=SUM(C15:D15)

Deleting rows, columns, and cells can play tricks on your formulas. Unless you are very experienced with Excel, you will want to double-check your formulas to make sure they perform as expected after the deletion.

QUICK REVIEW

Clearing and deleting are two common editing tasks in Excel. Clearing refers to removing information within a cell, while deleting refers to removing the entire cell from your sheet.

To clear information, select the cells you want to clear. Then press the DELETE key or choose Clear from the Edit menu (you can then choose what type of clearing you wish to perform).

To delete cells, select the cells (including entire rows or columns) you want to delete. Then choose Delete from the Edit menu. If you are asked how the remaining cells should be moved, make a choice.

How to Duplicate Cells

One of the common tasks in Excel is to duplicate cells, using a different formula in each of the duplicated cells. For instance, let's assume that you have the spreadsheet shown in Figure 8.7 partially completed, and you want to add the correct formulas for the **Balance** column.

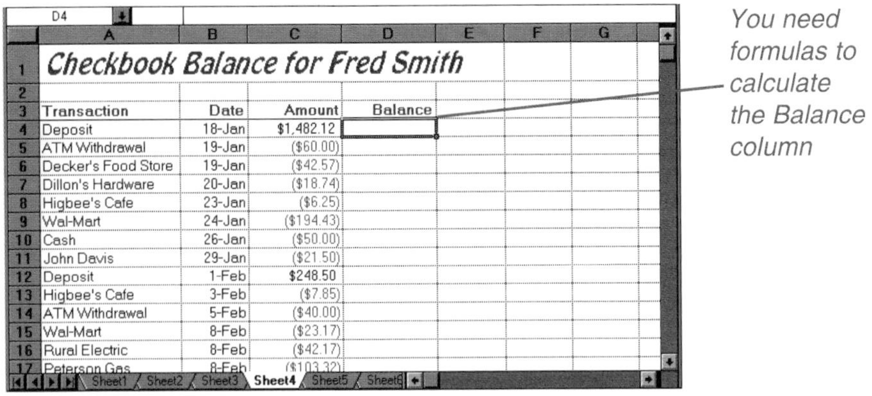

You need formulas to calculate the Balance column

Figure 8.7 Getting ready to duplicate cells.

There are two base formulas that you need to enter. The first is in the first cell of the balance column, which is D4. You know that at this point, the balance is equal to your first deposit. So, at D4 you can enter the following formula:

=C4

This simply indicates that D4 will be equal to C4, or your opening deposit of $1,482.12. Next, you need to enter a formula at D5 that indicates the balance after the next transaction. This is equal to your previous balance, plus the transaction (notice that the transaction amount is negative, so you *add* the transaction amount to the previous balance). To do this, select cell D5 and enter the following formula:

=D4 + C5

After entering this formula, your sheet will look like the one shown in Figure 8.8.

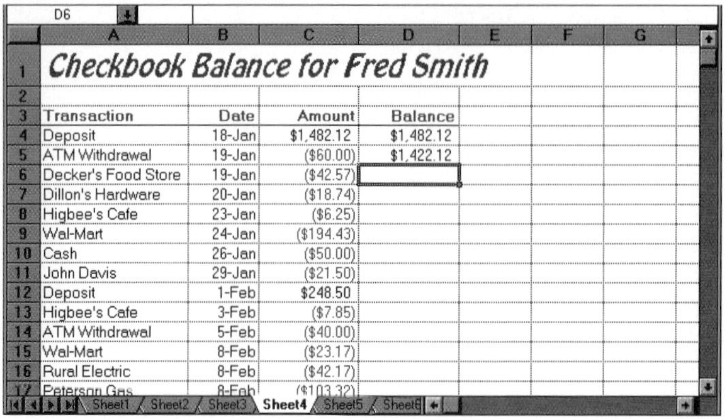

Figure 8.8 After entering the first two formulas.

The next step is a breeze, because all you need to do is duplicate the cell at D5 into the rest of the balance column. This is similar to the copy operation described at the first of this lesson, but it is a bit different, since you are copying from one cell into a range of cells.

First, make sure you select a range of cells in which the first cell is the last formula entered and the last cell is the last in the Balance column. For instance, you might select the range D5:D22. Then choose the Fill command from the Edit menu. You will then see the following submenu:

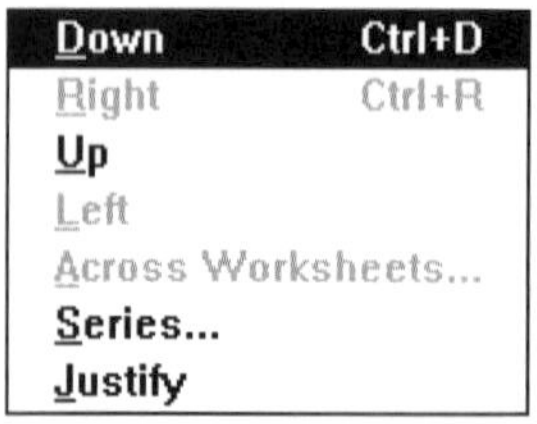

Excel is asking you which way you want to fill the range of cells you have selected. There are several options here, not all of which are available. (Certain options are made available based on the cell range you have selected.) The options on this submenu are detailed in Table 8.2.

Option	Function
Down	Copies the first cell in the range into the other cells in the range
Right	Copies the leftmost cell in the range into the other cells in the range

Table 8.2 Fill options and their functions. (continued on next page)

Option	Function
Up	Copies the bottom cell in the range into the other cells in the range
Left	Copies the rightmost cell in the range into the other cells in the range
Across Worksheets	Copies the selection to the same position on other sheets in the workbook
Series	Fills the cell range with a series of numbers or dates
Justify	Adjusts the text in the first cell so it does not exceed the column width, using as many cells in the range as necessary

Table 8.2 *Fill options and their functions. (continued from previous page)*

Notice that only the Down, Up, Series, and Justify options are available from the menu. Given the fact that the first cell in the range contains the formula you want to fill the range with, you should select the Down option. When you do this, Excel copies the formula to the rest of the range. Your Balance column is recalculated, and appears as shown in Figure 8.9.

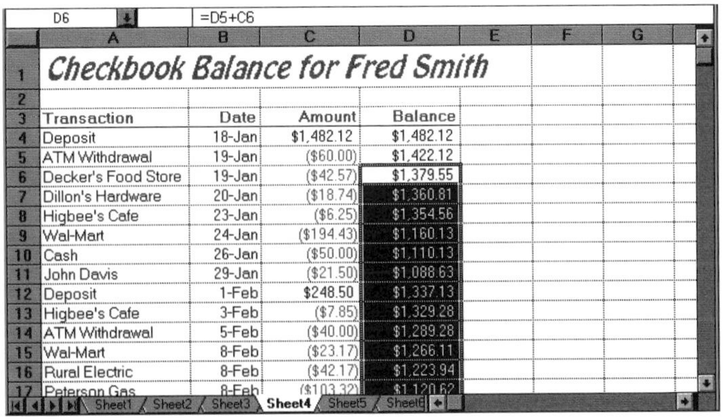

Figure 8.9 *After the duplication.*

This process works because of how Excel treats cell references. As you have learned throughout this lesson, when you move, copy, or delete anything, Excel tries to figure out how the references in the pasted formulas should appear. If they are absolute references, nothing is done to them. If they are relative references (as was the case in this example), an adjustment is made by Excel. In this case, the formula in each cell simply points to the one above it (the previous balance) and the one to the left (the transaction amount). When the formula is completed, a new balance is displayed.

WHAT YOU NEED TO KNOW

You have learned a lot of information in this lesson, but the techniques discussed here will be used time and again as you work with Excel. Specifically, you have learned the following:

☑ The difference between copying and cutting is that one leaves the original cells intact while the other does not.

☑ You can copy cells by first selecting them and then pressing CTRL-C, using the ▥ tool, or pressing CTRL-INSERT. Select where you want them pasted, and then press CTRL-V or use the ▥ tool.

☑ You can cut cells by first selecting them and then pressing CTRL-X or using the ✄ tool. Select where you want them pasted, and then press CTRL-V or use the ▥ tool.

☑ Clearing cells only removes the information within them; it does not delete the actual cells.

☑ You can delete cells by selecting what you want deleted, and then using the Delete command from the Edit menu. This command deletes entire cells, moving the surrounding cells to fill the void.

☑ When you cut, copy, or delete information, Excel makes adjustments to the remaining formulas in your sheet so they reflect the proper cell locations.

In the next lesson you will learn how to give meaningful names to a cell or block of cells and how to use these names.

Lesson 9

Using Names

Now that you know how to create workbooks and sheets, as well as how to work with formulas and functions, you can start to branch out a bit and make your life a little easier. This lesson covers using names to refer to different parts of your sheets. Specifically, you will learn how:

- Excel uses names
- To define a name
- To use names in formulas
- To use the formula bar to work with names
- To delete names

HOW EXCEL USES NAMES

We use names every day. They are words used to describe people, places, and things, and they make it easy to communicate with one another. Sometimes we use multiple names to refer to the same thing. For instance, you might refer to a box, a container, a receptacle, and a holder—all the time referring to the same item. It is the same way with Excel. You can use names to define specific portions of your spreadsheet; you can even use multiple names to refer to the same cell or range of cells.

When spreadsheets were first introduced, they didn't allow you to define names. It wasn't long before spreadsheet makers decided it was easier to refer to a name than a specific cell or range of cells. This makes sense—imagine how difficult it would be to refer to people by arbitrary numbers instead of names.

DEFINING NAMES

The first task in defining a name is to select the cells that you want associated with the name. For instance, take a look at the sheet shown in Figure 9.1. If you want to assign a name to the totals for each year, you can easily do so.

	A	B	C	D	E	F	G	H
		B16	±	=SUM(B4:B15)				
1								
2								
3	State	1991	1992	1993	3-Yr Growth			
4	Arkansas	9,743	15,162	25,226	158.91%			
5	Colorado	13,836	21,458	27,345	97.64%			
6	Florida	15,939	28,137	36,831	131.07%			
7	Georgia	48,540	50,915	56,741	16.90%			
8	Indiana	14,022	18,820	32,437	131.33%			
9	Kentucky	12,579	19,556	34,568	174.81%			
10	New York	21,817	37,672	41,901	92.06%			
11	Ohio	24,156	40,107	62,439	158.48%			
12	Oregon	17,968	22,291	34,568	92.39%			
13	Pennsylvania	23,021	24,917	43,813	90.32%			
14	Texas	36,049	43,325	51,574	43.07%			
15	Wyoming	12,336	16,210	23,143	87.61%			
16	Totals	250,006	338,570	470,586	88.23%			
17								
18								

Sheet1 / Sheet2 / Sheet3 / Sheet4 \ Sheet5 / Sheet6

Figure 9.1 A sample sheet.

To assign a name, first select the cell you want assigned to that name. In this example, select cell B16 (as shown in Figure 9.1). Then, choose the Name option from the Insert menu. You will then see the following submenu:

Define...
Paste...
Create...
Apply...

What you want to do is to define a name, so press ENTER to accept the highlighted choice, Define. Excel then displays the Define Name dialog box, shown in Figure 9.2:

Excel proposes a name here

A list of other names you have defined

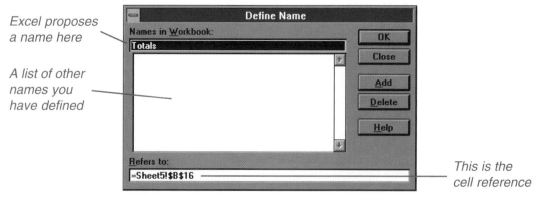

Define Name

Names in **W**orkbook:

Totals

OK

Close

Add

Delete

Help

Refers to:

=Sheet5!B16

This is the cell reference

Figure 9.2 The Define Name dialog box.

Notice that Excel is proposing that you use the name Totals. This is because it is the text just to the left of the cell you selected, and it is a good candidate for a name. Excel has no way of knowing that you plan on defining names for other numbers in this row, so all you need to do is supply a more descriptive name. For instance, you might enter the name **Total_1991.**

Names you supply in Excel must meet the following criteria:

- They must begin with a letter or an underscore.

- After the first character, they can contain any letters, numbers, or the underscore.

- They cannot have spaces in them (an underscore can serve that purpose).

- They must be less than 256 characters long.

When you have finished entering a name, press ENTER or click on ▮ OK ▮

The name is defined. You can now define the other names (Total_1992 and Total_1993) by moving to the appropriate cells and repeating this process. When you have finished, notice that Excel lets you know whenever you have selected a named cell. Typically, the formula bar contains the address of the cell you have selected. If the cell is named, the formula bar contains the name you defined for that cell.

The cell address appears here   *Unless the cell is named*

D15   Total_1993

USING A NAME IN A FORMULA

In Lesson 7 you learned how formulas extend the power and versatility of a spreadsheet program such as Excel. You can extend that versatility just a bit further by using names in formulas. As an example, let's go back to the sheet used in the last section. Suppose that you want to modify the formula shown in Figure 9.3 so that it uses names.

Note that the first step (as illustrated in Figure 9.3) is to select the cell that will contain the formula—the cell at E16. Since this cell already contains a formula, there are two ways you can convert it to use your newly defined names. The first method is to retype the formula. Since it is a short formula, this is perfectly acceptable. All you need to do is replace the current formula with the new one:

=(Total_1993 – Total_1991) / Total_1991

E16		=(D16-B16)/B16					
	A	B	C	D	E	F	G	H

	A	B	C	D	E
1					
2					
3	State	1991	1992	1993	3-Yr Growth
4	Arkansas	9,743	15,162	25,226	158.91%
5	Colorado	13,836	21,458	27,345	97.64%
6	Florida	15,939	28,137	36,831	131.07%
7	Georgia	48,540	50,915	56,741	16.90%
8	Indiana	14,022	18,820	32,437	131.33%
9	Kentucky	12,579	19,556	34,568	174.81%
10	New York	21,817	37,672	41,901	92.06%
11	Ohio	24,156	40,107	62,439	158.48%
12	Oregon	17,968	22,291	34,568	92.39%
13	Pennsylvania	23,021	24,917	43,813	90.32%
14	Texas	36,049	43,325	51,574	43.07%
15	Wyoming	12,336	16,210	23,143	87.61%
16	*Totals*	250,006	338,570	470,586	88.23%
17					
18					

Sheet1 / Sheet2 / Sheet3 / Sheet4 \ **Sheet5** / Sheet6

You want to change this formula

Figure 9.3 Getting ready to change the formula.

In a formula such as this, the use of names makes the formula much more meaningful and susceptible to less errors. This assumes, of course, that you type it correctly. If you have a long formula to retype, you have "fumble fingers" and might not type it correctly, or you have quite a few newly defined names, then you can use the second method of formula conversion. To do this, select the cell at E16 again. This time, however, you don't want to retype the formula. Instead, choose the Name option from the Insert menu. You will again see the submenu shown earlier, this time there with more options available:

Choose the Apply option. Using this option, you can automatically convert cell references into their appropriate names. When you choose the option, you will see the Apply Names dialog box, as shown in Figure 9.4:

In the Apply Names list, choose the names you want applied. Most of the time, you can select all of the names. To do this, simply click on each of the names in the list, until all of them have been highlighted. Then, press ENTER or click on █ OK █.

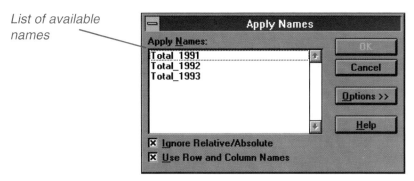

List of available
names

Figure 9.4 *The Apply Names dialog box.*

The appropriate cell references have now been replaced with the appropriate names, as shown in Figure 9.5.

Formula now uses names

	A	B	C	D	E	F	G	H
	E16		=(Total_1993-Total_1991)/Total_1991					
1								
2								
3	State	1991	1992	1993	3-Yr Growth			
4	Arkansas	9,743	15,162	25,226	158.91%			
5	Colorado	13,836	21,458	27,345	97.64%			
6	Florida	15,939	28,137	36,831	131.07%			
7	Georgia	48,540	50,915	56,741	16.90%			
8	Indiana	14,022	18,820	32,437	131.33%			
9	Kentucky	12,579	19,556	34,568	174.81%			
10	New York	21,817	37,672	41,901	92.06%			
11	Ohio	24,156	40,107	62,439	158.48%			
12	Oregon	17,968	22,291	34,568	92.39%			
13	Pennsylvania	23,021	24,917	43,813	90.32%			
14	Texas	36,049	43,325	51,574	43.07%			
15	Wyoming	12,336	16,210	23,143	87.61%			
16	Totals	250,006	338,570	470,586	88.23%			
17								

Sheet1 / Sheet2 / Sheet3 / Sheet4 \ **Sheet5** \ Sheet6

Figure 9.5 *The modified formula.*

In Lesson 8 you learned what happens to cell references in formulas when you add, delete, or move cells. The same process holds true with names. Formulas that use names will always point to the proper area, since Excel updates name references whenever you add, delete, or move cells.

JUMPING TO A NAME

Besides their use in formulas, you can also use names as a way of marking a portion of your sheet for quick access. Let's assume that you have a large sheet that is impossible to fit on a single page. Rather than searching through the entire sheet for a specific number, you can define a name to refer to the cell that contains the number. Then you can use the Go To option from the Edit menu (or press **F5**). You will see the Go To dialog box, as shown in Figure 9.6:

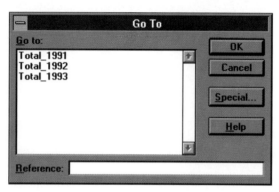

Figure 9.6 *The Go To dialog box.*

Choose the name you want to jump to and click on OK . Excel displays and selects the cell or range of cells associated with the name.

USING THE FORMULA BAR TO WORK WITH NAMES

You now know the basics of working with names. There are a couple more shortcuts you can use with Excel, however, that will help you to quickly use names. Both of these involve the use of the formula bar. One shortcut allows you to define names, while the other allows you to jump to them.

DEFINING WITH THE FORMULA BAR

Take a look at the left side of the formula bar. Notice that the cell address is located there:

Cell address

Use the mouse to click on the cell address; the address is highlighted. Now type the name you want applied to the cell or range of cells you have selected. Remember that you must follow the guidelines for names as listed earlier in this lesson. When you press ENTER, the name is defined.

JUMPING WITH THE FORMULA BAR

The formula bar also comes in handy for quickly doing jumps to existing names. First, click on the arrow to the right of the cell address on the formula bar. You will notice that Excel displays a drop-down list of names you have defined:

— Defined names

Select the name you want to jump to, and then press ENTER. Excel displays and selects the cell or cell range assigned to the name.

DELETING NAMES

There may come a time when you want to delete names you previously defined and used. To do this, simply choose Name from the Insert menu, and then choose Define. (I know; it sounds strange to choose Define when you really want to delete a name.) You will then see the Define Names dialog box, as shown in Figure 9.7:

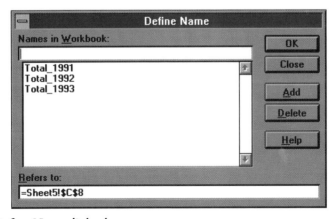

Figure 9.7 The Define Name dialog box.

In the list of existing names, select the one you want to delete; then click on the [Delete] button. The name is removed from the list, and the dialog box is still displayed. You can continue deleting (or defining) names, clicking on [OK] when you are finished.

WHAT YOU NEED TO KNOW

Using names can make your Excel sheets and workbooks easier to understand and maintain. Defining, using, and managing names is both easy and quick. In this lesson you have learned the following items:

- ☑ Excel allows you to assign names to either cells or a cell range. This aids in remember the purpose of the cells.

- ☑ Names are defined by selecting the cell or cells you want to name, and then selecting the Name option from the Insert menu. Select Define and provide the name you want to use.

- ☑ When creating formulas, you can use names in place of cell references or cell ranges. This makes your formulas much more meaningful and easy to maintain.

- ☑ Excel provides a shortcut, via the formula bar, for working with names.

- ☑ Once names are no longer needed, they can be deleted or reused again.

In the next lesson you will learn about array formulas and how to use them.

Lesson 10

Using Arrays in Formulas

So far you have learned quite a bit about formulas. You know how to enter them, use functions in them, edit them, and use names to make them more understandable. There is one other topic concerning formulas that you might want to learn. This has to do with *arrays*. Excel supports the use of arrays in formulas, allowing you to enter a single formula that produces multiple results. While this might sound confusing right now, hopefully by the end of this lesson you will have learned the following:

- How arrays differ from regular formulas

- How arrays are entered in Excel

- How you edit formulas containing arrays

HOW ARRAYS DIFFER FROM REGULAR FORMULAS

You already know what a regular formula is—it is a relationship between two cells that produces a result. For instance, the following is a simple formula:

=E7 * E8

This produces a single result which is derived by multiplying the contents of cell E7 by those in cell E8. You can, however, define an *array formula*, which produces multiple results. For instance, the following formula:

{=A7:E7 * A8:E8}

produces five results; it is the same as the following five formulas:

=A7 * A8
=B7 * B8
=C7 * C8
=D7 * D8
=E7 * E8

The reason that the array might be more attractive than the individual formulas is that you only need to enter it once—Excel then takes care of making the proper associations between elements of the array.

ENTERING ARRAY FORMULAS

To enter an array, you follow three steps:

1. Select the range of cells that will contain the resulting array.

2. Enter the formula as you would any regular Excel formula.

3. Press SHIFT-CTRL-ENTER to let Excel know this is an array.

When Excel displays the formula, it places braces around it. For instance, a normal formula might appear as:

$$=B2 + B3 \quad\text{------ Regular formula}$$

whereas an array formula appears as:

$$\{=A2:F2 + A3:F3\} \quad\text{------ Array Formula}$$

The braces are added by Excel automatically when you perform step 3, above. You do not need to type them yourself. This formula representation is shown in every cell of the range you selected in step 1, above.

As an example of how to enter an array, suppose you are working with the sheet shown in Figure 10.1:

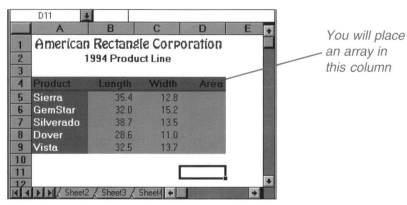

You will place an array in this column

Figure 10.1 Sample sheet.

You have your raw information, and you want to calculate the Area column. While you could do this using techniques described in previous lessons, you decide that you want to use an array.

The first step is to use your mouse to select cells D5:D9. This is the portion of the Area column that will receive the result of the array. Next, type the formula you want to use to calculate this column:

=B5:B9 * C5:C9

Don't press ENTER or move to any other cell yet. Instead, press SHIFT-CTRL-ENTER. The array result is placed in cells D5:D9, and the formula appears in the formula bar—it is the same formula you typed, except it is enclosed in braces. The same formula appears in every cell of D5:D9. the result of the array looks like Figure 10.2:

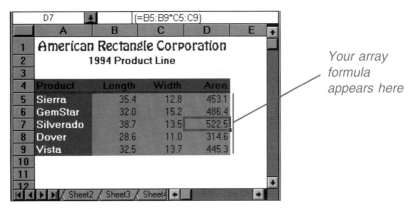

Figure 10.2 Sample sheet with new column.

EDITING ARRAYS

Since arrays are only entered once, yet their results occupy multiple cells, you cannot edit them in the same manner as regular formulas. The actions you take to edit an array depend on what you want to do. Changing the array formula is the easiest to do, whereas performing other editing tasks, such as deleting, clearing, or moving the array, take a bit more work.

CHANGING AN ARRAY FORMULA

Changing an array formula is very easy. All you need to do is select any cell in the array and then use the editing techniques described in Lesson 6. If you try to simply press ENTER when you are through with your edit, you will receive an error message like that shown in Figure 10.3:

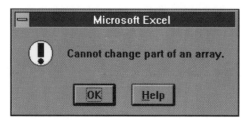

Figure 10.3 *An Error message dialog box.*

This is because Excel assumes you are trying to change only the one cell you have selected. You need to change the entire array formula. This is signified by pressing CTRL-SHIFT-ENTER—the same as you did when you first entered the formula. When you do this, the entire array formula is changed.

PERFORMING OTHER EDITS

To delete, clear, or move cells that are part of an array, you cannot work with individual cells in the array. For instance, if you tried to clear cell D7, shown earlier, Excel would display the error notice you just read. Instead, you must select the entire array before you can edit it. This is easy to do if you remember the cell range you used for the original array. This is not always the case, however. Instead, you can use the Go To command. This command was first described in Lesson 9, but not in relation to arrays.

First, select a cell you know resides within the array you want to edit. Then, choose the Go To command from the Edit menu. When you select this command and see the Go To dialog box (see Lesson 9 if you need a refresher), you should click on the Special... button. When you do, you will see the Go To Special dialog box, as shown in Figure 10.4. Click on the Current Array option and then the OK button. Excel selects the entire array for you.

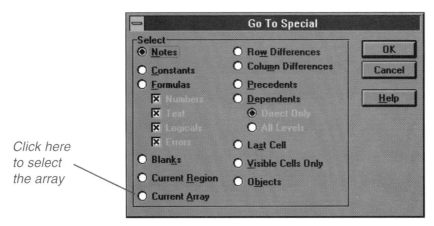

Click here
to select
the array

Figure 10.4 The Go To Special dialog box.

Once the array is selected, you can perform edit such as deleting, clearing, or moving. These are performed in the same manner described earlier in this book.

WHAT YOU NEED TO KNOW

Arrays can be powerful, important time savers when you are creating your workbooks. Arrays allow you to enter a formula once, and have it applied to an entire range of cells. In this lesson you have learned how array formulas can be used. If you plan on using arrays, you need to know at least the following information:

- ☑ An array formula allows you to define multiple relationships with a single formula.

- ☑ You enter an array by selecting the cell range in which you want the results to appear, entering the formula (using cell ranges on both sides of the operator) and then pressing SHIFT-CTRL-ENTER.

- ☑ Since array formulas are a bit different than regular formulas, you use different techniques to edit them.

In the next lesson you will learn about the commands that save your workbook to disk, both manually and automatically and about keeping backup copies of your work.

Lesson 11

Saving Your Sheet

Now that you know the basics about how to create, edit, and manipulate workbooks and sheets, it is time to save your work. Saving workbooks and sheets is an important function. If you don't save them, you can't load them and work on them or print them at a later time. In this lesson, you will focus on how to save your work, while Lesson 12 covers how to load them. Specifically, this lesson covers

- Commands you can use to save workbooks

- Different methods of saving a workbook

- How to save your work automatically

- Forcing Excel to make backup copies of a workbook

THE COMMANDS THAT SAVE YOUR WORK

Excel provides three different commands to save your sheets. These commands are available from the File menu:

Save	Ctrl+S
Save As...	
Save Workspace...	

Each of these commands has a special purpose and will be explained in the following sections.

THE SAVE COMMAND

The Save option from the File menu is used to save your work to disk. It is effectively the same as clicking on the ▣ tool from the standard toolbar. This command does not give you the opportunity to name your file; it simply saves it to disk. If your sheet is unnamed (you haven't saved your new sheet yet), the Save command functions the same as the Save As command, which is described in the next section.

If you are saving a large file, Excel will display a gauge on the status bar indicating what percentage of the file has been saved.

THE SAVE AS COMMAND

The Save As command is used whenever you want to save your sheet to a brand new filename, directory, or drive. When you choose this command, you will see the Save As dialog box, as shown in Figure 11.1:

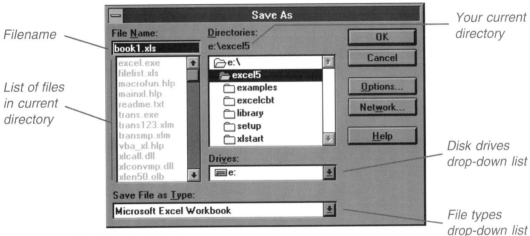

Figure 11.1 The Save As dialog box.

If you are familiar with other Windows products, you will have no problem using this dialog box. All you need to do is change the directory or disk drive (if desired), and specify a filename. By default, Excel sheet files use the XLS filename extension. When you press ENTER or click on the OK button, your sheet is saved to the file you specified.

You only need to use the Save As command when you first save a sheet or when you want to change the filename, directory, or drive used for the sheet. If you are working with a sheet that has already been saved once, you can just use the Save command. It is much quicker than using the Save As command—it doesn't call up a dialog box.

THE SAVE WORKSPACE COMMAND

As you will learn later in this book (Lesson 32), you can open multiple workbooks in Excel, and view more than one workbook at a time. If you are working with many different files, and you have spent a great deal of time setting up your work area, you can use the Save Workspace command so that your efforts are not lost when you later exit Excel. Unlike the other save commands, this command also stores information about which files were open and how much of the screen each consumed.

When you choose Save Workspace from the File menu, you will see the Save Workspace dialog box, shown in Figure 11.2, which is very similar to the Save As dialog box shown earlier:

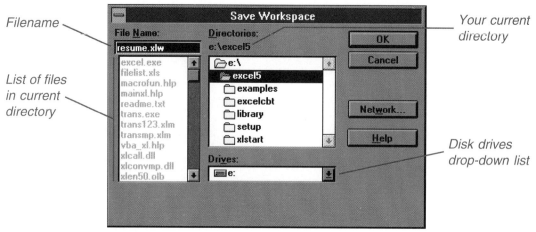

Figure 11.2 The Save Workspace dialog box.

Excel saves workspace files with the XLW filename extension; the filename RESUME.XLW is the suggested default filename. In effect, this file, when loaded again, allows you to resume your work exactly where you left off.

AUTOMATICALLY SAVING YOUR WORK

If you sit at your computer and use Excel for hours on end, you know it is easy to get so wrapped up in your work that you forget to save your workbook. This can be very dangerous, since you could lose your work if the power goes out or the program freezes for some reason. (One of the corollaries to Murphy's law states that the power will always go out 15 seconds before you save your work.)

Excel provides an add-in (a program addition) that allows you to save your workbook automatically, at any interval you desire. Thus, you will not need to remember to save your work. Instead, you can concentrate on the content of your sheet.

To instruct Excel to save your work automatically, choose AutoSave from the Tools menu. If this option is not available from the Tools menu, you need to enable this special add-in. To do this, select Add-Ins from the Tools menu. When you do this, you will see the Add-ins dialog box, as shown in Figure 11.3:

An x here selects AutoSave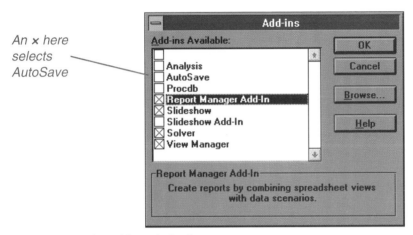

Figure 11.3 The Add-ins dialog box.

Make sure the AutoSave add-in is selected, then click on [OK]. Now you can choose the AutoSave option from the Tools menu. You will then see the AutoSave dialog box, shown in Figure 11.4:

Click here to turn automatic saving on or off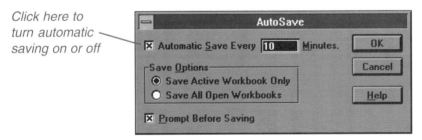

Figure 11.4 The AutoSave dialog box.

To enable automatic saving, make sure an x appears in the check box for the Automatic Save option. The control box should then display the number of minutes after which Excel will save your work. This is an interval time period and represents how frequently your work is saved. If you want to use a different interval, simply change the number using either the up arrow or down arrow to the right of the number or by entering a number with the keyboard. You can specify any interval between one minute and 32,767 minutes (22 days, 18 hours, 7 minutes).

As you are working, the AutoSave add-in keeps track of how many minutes it has been since the last time you saved your work. When you reach the interval you assigned, and your work still has not been saved, Excel displays a dialog box, as shown in Figure 11.5, asking if you want to save:

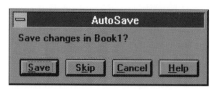

Figure 11.5 Dialog box seen when the AutoSave interval is reached.

KEEPING BACKUP COPIES OF YOUR WORK

Backup copies, by definition, are simply the file as it was previously saved. Thus, if you save your workbook, the old workbook file is renamed to have the BAK extension, and the current sheet is saved in the workbook file with the XLS extension. In this way you always have at least one older generation of your workbook to fall back on, if necessary.

The only problem with making backup copies is that they can occupy quite a bit of disk space. If you have backup copies for all your workbooks, you effectively double the amount of disk space necessary for the files. Many people find this unacceptable, so Excel, by default, does not make backup copies of your workbooks. If you want to force Excel to make backup copies, you must do so on a workbook-by-workbook basis. When you first save a file, you recall from the first part of this lesson that you see the Save As dialog box. From this dialog box, choose the Options... button. When you do, you will see the Save Options dialog box, as shown in Figure 11.6:

Controls backup copies

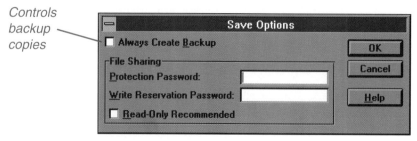

Figure 11.6 The Save Options dialog box.

The first option on the dialog box is Always Create Backup. Ensure that there is an ∞ in the check box to the left of this option, and Excel will make backup copies of this workbook every time you save it. Remember that this is for this workbook only; if you want to force Excel to make backup copies of your other workbooks, you must go through this same process for each of them.

WHAT YOU NEED TO KNOW

Excel provides many different ways you can save your workbooks. When you are using the program, sooner or later you will need to save your work. (This is, of course, unless you don't care about saving your workbooks after each work session.)

In this lesson you have learned the following:

- ☑ Saving frequently will prevent a lot of pain.
- ☑ You use the Save As command to save a new file or save an existing file to a new name, drive, or directory.
- ☑ You use the Save command to save recent changes to a previously saved file.
- ☑ You can use the Save Workspace command to save exactly how your screen looks.
- ☑ You can instruct Excel to save your work at set intervals.
- ☑ You can force Excel to make backup copies of individual workbooks.

Once you have saved your workbook, the assumption is that you will need to load (open) it again. Loading your workbooks is covered in Lesson 12.

Lesson 12

Loading Your Workbook

In Lesson 11 you learned how to save your workbook. One of the basic necessities of a program (particularly a program like Excel) is the ability to save and, at a later time, reload (open) your work. In this lesson you will learn how to

- Load your Excel workbooks
- Load different types of files
- Search for files

LOADING AN EXCEL WORKBOOK

In Excel, loading a workbook is referred to as *opening a workbook* or *opening a file.* This is done in one of two ways. First, you can use the Open command from the File menu. Second, you can use the ![tool] tool on the toolbar. No matter which method you use to load a file, you will see the Open dialog box, as shown in Figure 12.1:

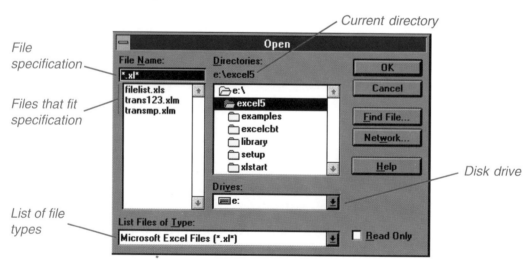

Figure 12.1 The Open dialog box.

If you are familiar with any other Windows programs that use files, this dialog box might look familiar. The simplest way to use it is to just select a workbook file and press ENTER or click on the `OK` button. Alternatively, you could simply double-click on the filename. If you wish, you can specify other directories or disk drives from which you wish to load a workbook.

When you instruct Excel to load a file, it reads the file contents into memory so you can either edit or print the file. The original file remains on the disk; it is not changed. Any changes you make occur only in the computer's memory. You should remember to save any changes (as you learned in Lesson 11) if you want those changes to be permanent.

SELECTING OTHER FILES

By default, Excel displays only Excel files when you choose to open a file. Excel files include any of those shown in Table 12.1.

Extension	Type of File
XLS	Workbook file
XLC	Chart file
XLM	Macro file
XLW	Workspace file

Table 12.1 Files used by Excel.

However, you can also instruct Excel to load different types of files. There are two ways to do this. The simplest method is to specify a different file type in the List Files of Type field at the bottom of the Open dialog box. When you click on the arrow to the right of this field, you will see a list of commonly used files that Excel understands, as shown in Figure 12.2.

Select one of these, and Excel displays only those types of files in the file list. If you instruct Excel to display all files, you will see all files in the current directory.

The other way to view different files is to enter a file specification in the File Name field at the top of the file list. This is essentially all that Excel does. It displays all the Excel files when the file specification is set to *.XL*. If you choose to display all the files in the directory, set the file specification to *.*. You can use any file specification you desire.

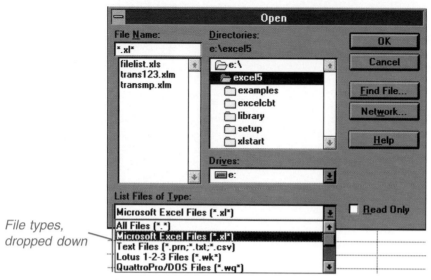

File types,
dropped down

Figure 12.2 *The Open dialog box with the File Types list dropped down.*

The file specification you use must adhere to DOS file-specification rules. This means that you can use any legal filename characters, along with the question mark (?) and asterisk (*) wildcard characters. The question mark is used as a placeholder for a single character, while an asterisk is used as a placeholder one or more characters. If you need additional information on wildcard characters, refer to the book *Rescued by DOS*, Jamsa Press, 1993.

Once you have displayed the file list as you like it (by using the two methods just described), you can load a specific file using the same steps covered in the previous section.

QUICKLY LOADING YOUR MOST RECENT WORKBOOKS

Many people who work with Excel work with the same workbooks over and over again. For instance, you might be working on a financial report for work, and that work covers a period of several weeks. Every time you use Excel, you load this same file and continue working and refining your thoughts. If you find yourself in this situation, it is bothersome to repeatedly go through the steps necessary to opening the file.

Excel provides a shortcut you can use to sidestep this hassle. Take a look at the File menu, as shown in Figure 12.3:

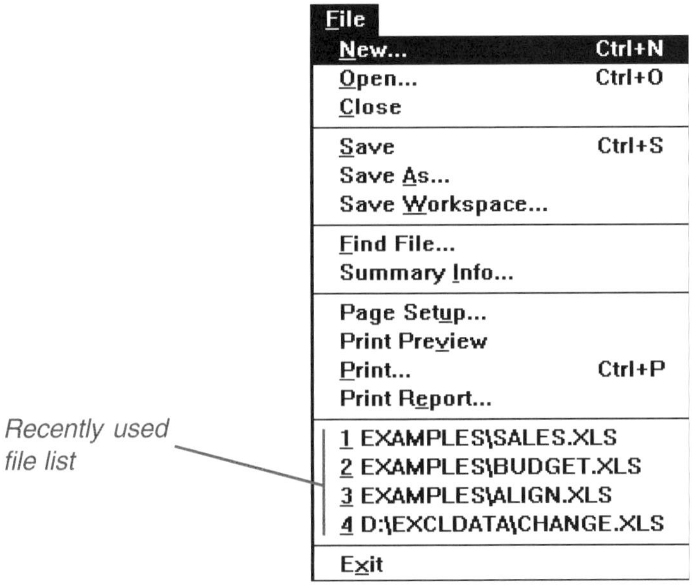

File	
New...	Ctrl+N
Open...	Ctrl+O
Close	
Save	Ctrl+S
Save As...	
Save Workspace...	
Find File...	
Summary Info...	
Page Setup...	
Print Preview	
Print...	Ctrl+P
Print Report...	
1 EXAMPLES\SALES.XLS	
2 EXAMPLES\BUDGET.XLS	
3 EXAMPLES\ALIGN.XLS	
4 D:\EXCLDATA\CHANGE.XLS	
Exit	

Recently used file list

Figure 12.3 *The File menu, dropped down.*

Notice that there are four files listed at the bottom of the menu. These are the four most recent files that you have loaded (number 1 being the most recent). Thus, they represent the last work you did with Excel. If you want to load a file you used in your previous Excel session, you can simply pull down the File menu and select the file you want to use. From the keyboard, you can press ALT-F and then the number to the left of the file you want.

If you do not see the file list at the bottom of the file menu, it may be that someone has disabled this feature of Excel. To turn it on, you should select Options from the Tools menu. You will then see the Options dialog box. Make sure you select the General file card, and the Options dialog box will appear, as shown in Figure 12.4. In the Menus box, make sure the option titled Recently Used File List is selected.

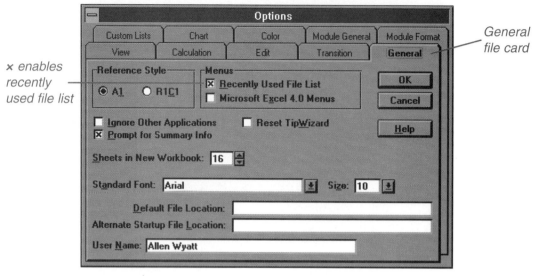

Figure 12.4 The Options dialog box showing the General file card.

QUICK REVIEW

Unless you want to redo your work every time you start Excel, it is imperative that you know how to load files. To load an Excel file (or any other file that can be imported by Excel), follow one of these steps:

- Choose Open from the File menu, then select a file from the Open dialog box.

- Choose a recently used file from the list at the bottom of the File menu.

- Click on ☑, then select a file from the Open dialog box.

FINDING YOUR FILES

As you work with Excel over an extended period, it is possible to create many, many files. Chances are that you have several versions of some of these workbooks. If you haven't worked with a workbook in a while, it is very easy to forget the workbook's filename. So how do you locate it again?

The easiest way is to use the Find File capability built into Excel. This can be accessed in one of two ways. First, you can select Find File from the File menu. Second, you can click on the `Find File...` button in the Open dialog box.

The dialog box you see next depends on whether you have used the Find File feature before. If you have not, you will see the Search dialog box, shown in Figure 12.5:

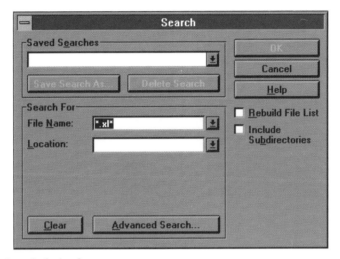

Figure 12.5 The Search dialog box.

If you have, you are taken directly to the Find File dialog box (discussed shortly) and shown the results of your last file search. Click on the ⬚Search... button to bring up the Search dialog box. The Find File feature of Excel is very powerful. You can use it to search for files in a specific drive or directory. Explaining the full use of this feature is far beyond the scope of this book. However, it is helpful for you to know how to use Find File to look for a workbook.

Only a few fields in the Search dialog box are of any consequence when doing a simple file search. Excel allows you to perform much more detailed searches, however, by clicking on the ⬚Advanced Search... button. You won't need to do that most of the time, and there is no need to do it right now. For most searches, you can simply fill in the information on the regular Search dialog box.

The most commonly used fields on the Search dialog box are the File Name and Location fields. In the File Name field you can provide a file specification, using the same techniques you learned earlier in this lesson. In the Location field you indicate where you want Excel to search. When you click on the arrow to the right of the Location field, you can select individual drives or directories you want to search.

As an example of how to use Find File quickly, let's suppose you want to search drive C for all of your workbook files. Enter *.**XLS** in the File Name field and choose **C:** in the Location field. To search all directories on drive C, select the check box to the left of the Include Subdirectories label.

When you have finished providing the search specification, click on the [OK] button. Excel reads the drives and directories you have specified, looking for files that meet your criteria. These files are then displayed in the Find File dialog box, shown in Figure 12.6.

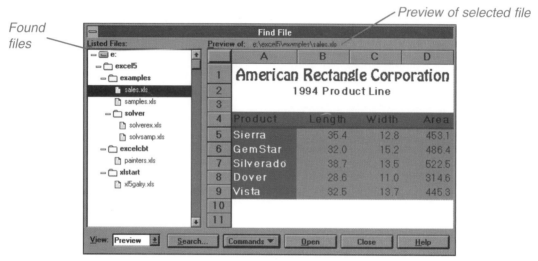

*Figure 12.6 Results of *.XLS search, with selected file previewed.*

Notice that the left side of the Find File dialog box displays a list of files located in the search, regardless of the directory in which they were located. To the right side of the dialog box is information about the highlighted file. You can control which information is shown in this part of the dialog box by clicking on the View field in the lower-left corner of the dialog box. Chances are you will want the content of your files displayed, so leave the field set to Preview.

You can display different files by using the arrow keys or the mouse to select different files from the file list. You can then browse through these files and perform other searches, as desired. When you have located the file you want, click on [Open], and Excel will open the file for you.

WHAT YOU NEED TO KNOW

This lesson has covered a lot of ground, particularly in the last section. Excel allows you to load all types of spreadsheet files—even those that were not created by Excel. In this lesson you have learned the following:

☑ You load an Excel workbook by using the tool or by using the Open command from the File menu.

☑ Besides workbook files, you can also load charts, macros, and workspace files directly into Excel.

☑ Excel allows you to load spreadsheet files created by different programs such as Lotus 1-2-3 or QuattroPro.

☑ You can quickly load a file you recently worked on by choosing the file name from the bottom of the File menu.

☑ The Find File feature of Excel allows you to quickly find, review, and load a file from disk.

These skills, particularly the skill of finding lost files, are extremely useful when using Excel. You will need to practice finding files, but over time you will be able to use the loading features of Excel with no problem at all.

In the next lesson you will learn about printing your workbook.

Lesson 13

Printing Your Workbook

A spreadsheet program (Excel included) would be of little value if it did not allow you to print what you spend so may hours working on—your sheets and workbooks. Printing is, typically, the end result of any workbook you create. This lesson provides you with the information you need in order to

- Select your printer

- Use Print Preview to see your workbook before printing it

- Print your workbook easily and quickly

- Print a single copy of your workbook

This lesson deals with printing your spreadsheet data—your sheets and workbooks. If you are interested in printing charts created with Excel, refer to Section 5, particularly to Lesson 29.

SETTING UP YOUR PRINTER

Excel works with whatever printers you have set up in Windows. Adding printer drivers and configuring Windows to work with your printers is beyond the scope of this book. For more information in this area, refer to *Rescued by Windows,* Jamsa Press, 1993.

One of the important things you can do in Excel (and the first step you should perform prior to printing) is to make sure you have the proper printer selected for your output. If you have only one printer, this step will not be necessary. Only when you have installed more than one printer driver with Windows will you need to do this.

To specify which printer you want Excel to use, select Print from the File menu. You will then see the Print dialog box, shown in Figure 13.1:

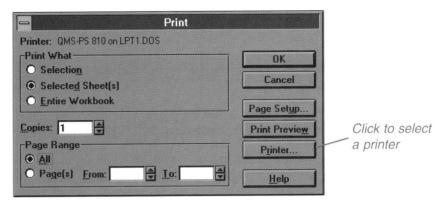

Figure 13.1 The Print dialog box.

From this dialog box, you should choose the [Printer...] button. This results in the display of the Print Setup dialog box, which will look something like Figure 13.2:

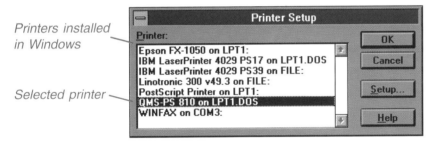

Figure 13.2 The Printer Setup dialog box.

The list of printers shown in your dialog box will differ from those shown here, but they will match the printers you have defined within Windows. Highlight the printer you want to use and then click on [OK]. You are returned to the Print dialog box.

USING PRINT PREVIEW

How many times have you printed information, only to find some little thing wrong? You make the correction and print again. In some instances, you might print the same information several times before it is just right. Excel provides a tool you can use so you don't have to waste so much paper in producing your final output. This tool is called Print Preview.

When you choose the Print Preview option from the File menu, or use the 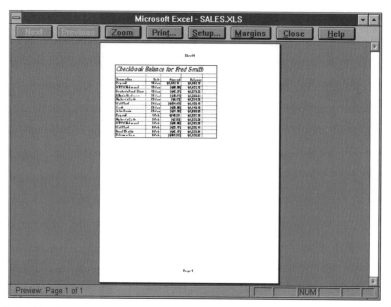 tool from the standard toolbar, what you see on your screen will change significantly. Any toolbars will disappear (to provide more screen space), and you will see an exact representation of how your printed workbook will look, as shown in Figure 13.3.

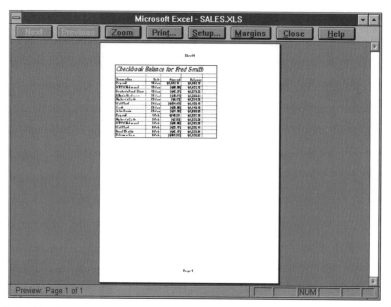

Figure 13.3 Print Preview.

Notice that a new button bar, specific to Print Preview, appears at the top of your screen. The tools on this toolbar allow you to control what you see (the zoom button) and make adjustments in margins and layout. If you have more than one page in your workbook, you can page through them by pressing the PGUP or PGDN keys on your keyboard (if your printout has only one page, they'll do nothing but beep) or using the scroll bars. When you have finished and you want to return to normal editing, press ESC or click on the Close button.

The legibility and value of the Print Preview tool will depend, in large part, on the quality and size of the monitor you are using with your computer. If you have a larger monitor and you are using Windows in a high resolution, then you might be able to read most of the type on the Print Preview display. If you are using a smaller monitor at a lower resolution, however, you will probably only be able to make out the largest type in your workbook.

SENDING YOUR WORKBOOK TO THE PRINTER

When it is finally time to print your workbook, you do this by using the Print option from the File menu. You will then see the Print dialog box, shown in Figure 13.4:

Printer to
be used

What to print

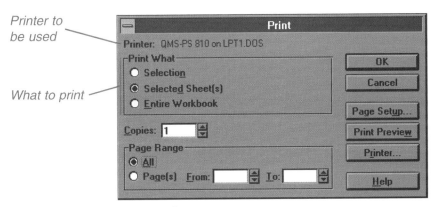

Figure 13.4 The Print dialog box.

The information at the top of this dialog box indicates where your workbook will be printed. If this is not the printer you want to use, choose a different printer, as described earlier in this lesson.

The actual information and options available from the Print dialog box can vary, depending on the type of printer you are using. Different printers have different capabilities, and Windows takes advantage of these capabilities as much as possible. In general, however, you can use this dialog box to select the number of copies you want to print and which pages you want to print.

One of the other things you can specify is what you want sent to the printer. This is done making a selection in the Print What box. By default, this field is set to Selected Sheet(s), typically meaning that only the current sheet will be printed. By changing this field, you can also specify that only a Selection (a cell range) be printed or that your entire Workbook is to be printed.

When you are satisfied with what you want to print, click on the ⬛ OK ⬛ button or press ENTER. Excel will send your information to the printer, as you have directed.

PRINTING A SINGLE COPY OF YOUR WORKBOOK QUICKLY

Most of the time, you will want to print only one copy of your workbook. Excel provides a quick way you can do this, using the ⬛ tool. When you click on this button, it is the same as choosing the Print command from the File menu and immediately clicking on OK.

Using the ⬛ tool results in one copy of your entire workbook being printed. If you need more than one copy or you want to print only a portion of your workbook, you must use the Print command as described in the previous section.

WHAT YOU NEED TO KNOW

Printing is, most of the time, a necessity with a spreadsheet program. With Excel, printing is a strength. This is because the program makes extensive and effective use of the printer drivers built into Windows. Once you have selected your printer, printing your workbook is very quick and easy. In this lesson you have learned some of the techniques you can use to print your workbook. The skills you should have learned include these:

- ☑ Selecting a printer only needs to be done when you first use Excel, if you have multiple printers available to your system, or if you think someone may have changed the printer before you used Excel.

- ☑ Using the Print Preview function from the File menu will save you time and paper. It shows you what your sheet will look like when printed.

- ☑ Printing is accomplished either by choosing Print from the File menu or by clicking on the ⬛ tool.

- ☑ Print a single copy of your workbook

In the next section you will begin to learn how you can format your workbook. Formatting allows you to control how your printed output will appear.

Section Three

FORMATTING YOUR WORKBOOK

Formatting refers to the process of adjusting the appearance of the information in your workbook. Excel allows you to separate content (the information in your workbook) completely from appearance (the format of this information). You can change and rechange how your information appears until you are entirely satisfied with the overall appearance of your workbook. Excel lets you change the formatting at the individual character level, the cell level, or at the sheet level. This section will teach you how you can make your workbook look the best it can.

Lesson 14

How Numbers Are Displayed

The base judgment of any spreadsheet is how well and easily it allows you to work with numbers. Excel has excellent number-handling functions and commands, and you can display those numbers in any manner desired. In this lesson you will learn how you can control the way in which Excel displays numbers. Specifically, you will learn how to

- Format numbers quickly
- Adjust the number of decimal points for a number
- Use predefined number formats
- Design custom number formats
- Use fractional formats

How Excel Handles Numbers

Internally, Excel handles all numbers the same. No matter how they look on your sheet, they are all treated as real numbers (having a value to the right of the decimal place) with up to 15 digits of precision.

That is internally. Externally, you can define exactly how you want your numbers displayed. By default, Excel displays numbers in a general format, meaning that they are shown exactly as they are entered. One, two, three, or more decimal places—it doesn't matter. However the number was entered, that is how Excel displays it.

Using Predefined Number Formats

If you don't like the way that Excel displays your numbers, you can change it. All you need to do is select the cells whose display you want to change. Then select the Cells option from the Format menu. You will see the Format Cells dialog box—make sure that the Number file card is displayed, as shown in Figure 14.1:

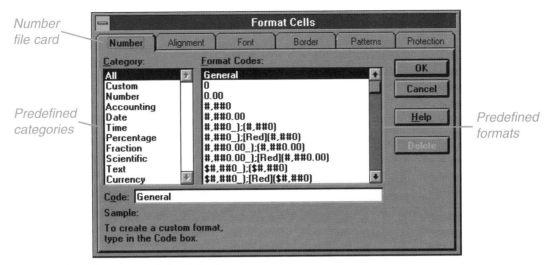

Number file card

Predefined categories

Predefined formats

Figure 14.1 The Format Cells dialog box.

Excel is provided with 43 different predefined number formats. As you can tell from the format category list at the left side of the dialog box, these formats are grouped into nine different categories. You can select any category you desire and then select a format from within that category.

Notice at the bottom of the dialog box there are two fields. One is entitled **Code**, and the other is **Sample**. The Code field is used to define custom number formats, as described later in this lesson. The Sample field is used to display what your number looks like in the selected number format. You should note that the Sample field will only have meaning if you have a number in the selected cell before you display the Format Cells dialog box. When you have finished choosing a number format, click on the OK button. The format is applied to every cell you have selected.

FORMATTING NUMBERS QUICKLY

If you want to change how a number in a certain cell is displayed quickly, you don't need to go through the trouble of using the Cells command from the Format menu. Instead, you can use buttons on the formatting toolbar. The three most common types of numeric formats are available as tools on the toolbar.

If you are working with financial figures, you might want to format your display with the currency button (⬛). Clicking here automatically formats a number with two decimal places, a leading dollar sign, and commas between the thousands. In addition, negative numbers will be shown in red, with brackets around them.

The next tool is allows you to format percentages. The ▨ button formats a number with a trailing % sign. In addition, the number appears to have been multiplied by 100. Thus, if the actual number is 1.23 and you format it as a percentage, it will be displayed as 123%.

The final numeric format that can be applied with the formatting toolbar is the comma format. This is done with the ▨ button, and actually applies a format from the Number category (on the left of the Format Cells dialog box). This results in the number having commas between the thousands, two decimal places, and negatives in red with parentheses.

While these three formats may not seem like much, they do make the most popular of the predefined formats available at the click of a button.

QUICKLY ADJUSTING THE NUMBER OF DECIMAL PLACES

You can also use the formatting toolbar to adjust quickly the number of decimal places used in a format. In the previous section you learned how you can use the three number tools on the formatting toolbar to specify how you want a number displayed. Just to the right of these tools are two other tools, which allow you to adjust how many decimal places are shown.

If you click on the ▨ button, the number of decimal places will increase. Thus, if the previous format used one decimal place, now two will be used. You can continue to add decimal places as long as you click on the button. Conversely, you can use the ▨ button to decrease the number of decimal places.

CREATING CUSTOM NUMBER FORMATS

So far in this lesson you have learned how to apply predefined number formats provided by Excel. You can, however, define your own formats. Take another look at the Format Cells dialog box. You can see in the Format Codes list that there are some pretty awesome looking codes—they can appear downright intimidating!

Don't despair; in this section you will learn how to read these codes so that you can create your own number formats. If you understand how to do this, you can easily read the formatting codes used in the Format Cells dialog box.

To create your own formatting code, select the Cells option from the Format menu. You will see the Format Cells dialog box; make sure that the Number file card is displayed, as shown in Figure 14.2:

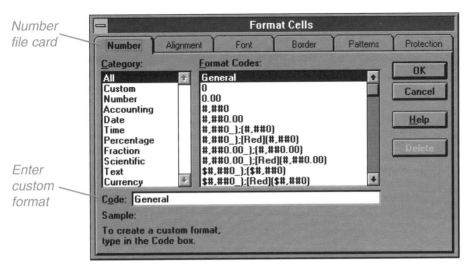

Number file card

Enter custom format

Figure 14.2 The Format Cells dialog box.

All you need to do is use any of the more than 40 formatting codes to create your own format. Enter this format in the Code field and then select the OK button. Your new format is used to display the value in the cells you had selected.

Excel supports quite a few different formatting codes for numbers. These formatting codes can generally be broken down into number formatting codes, date and time formatting codes, and conditional or color codes. The following sections describe each of these categories.

NUMBER FORMATTING CODES

Excel provides many formatting codes you can use to control how your numbers are displayed. If you don't see the exact format you need in one of the predefined formats, you can create your own. For instance, some codes you could create are shown in Table 14.1:

Format	Value	Displayed As
000-00-0000	296535653	296-53-5653
"ID "00/000	12345	ID 12/345
0.000%	.9876	98.760%

Table 14.1 Sample formatting codes.

The best way to discover how formatting codes can be used is to study how they are used in the predefined formats. Then you can experiment on your own to create your own formats. Table 14.2 lists the available formatting codes for numbers.

Symbol	Meaning
General	Uses the general display format described earlier in this lesson.
#	Used to indicate a single-digit position. The digit is only displayed if there is a digit in that position.
0	Used to indicate a single-digit position. If there is no digit in the position, a 0 is displayed.
?	Same as the 0 symbol, except results in a space being displayed for insignificant 0s on either side of the decimal point.
. (period)	The decimal point.
%	Percentage. The number is multiplied by 100 and the % sign is added, as described earlier in this lesson.
, (comma)	Thousands separator (if surrounded by digit place holders) or a thousands scaler (if the comma follows all the place holders).
E– E+ e– e+	Displays in scientific format.
$ – / ( ) : space	Displays that character
\	Forces display of the following character
*	Repeats the next character to fill out the column width.
_ (underscore)	Leaves a space the width of the following character.
"text"	Displays the text within the quotes.
@	Text place holder.

Table 14.2 Excel number formatting codes.

DATE AND TIME FORMATTING CODES

In Excel, dates and times are stored internally as numbers. These are only converted to readable dates and times when you format the cell using a date or time format. While there are predefined formats for all the common methods of displaying dates and times, there may be special cases where you want to create your own formats. For example, you can use the date and time formatting codes to create your own formats as shown in Table 14.3:

Format	Displayed As
"Today is "mmmm d, yyyy	Today is December 4, 1993
[h]:mm:ss	32:12:08
m/yy	2/94

Table 14.3 Date formatting code samples.

Table 14.4 lists the formatting codes that are specific to dates and times. You should also remember that you can also use many of the number formatting codes shown earlier in Table 14.2 (for instance, the period or those codes that cause specific characters to be displayed).

Symbol	Meaning
m	Displays the month or minutes as a number without a leading 0
mm	Displays the month or minutes as a number with a leading 0
mmm	Displays the month as abbreviated text (Jan, Feb, Mar, etc.)
mmmm	Displays the month as text (January, February, March, etc.)
d	Displays the day of the month as a number without a leading 0
dd	Displays the day of the month as a number with a leading 0
ddd	Displays the day of the week as abbreviated text (Sun, Mon, Tue, etc.)
dddd	Displays the day of the week as text (Sunday, Monday, Tuesday, etc.)
yy	Displays the year with two digits
yyyy	Displays the year with four digits
h	Displays the hour without a leading 0
hh	Displays the hour with a leading 0
s	Displays the seconds with a leading 0
ss	Displays the seconds without a leading 0
[ ]	When surrounding hours, minutes, or seconds place holders, displays hours greater than 24 or minutes and seconds greater than 60
AM am PM pm A a P p	Uses a 12-hour clock, displaying AM or PM as specified

Table 14.4 *Excel number-formatting codes for dates and times.*

ADDING COLORS OR CONDITIONALS TO NUMBER FORMATS

In the previous two sections you learned how you can use formatting codes to display numbers, dates, and times. Excel also allows you to include formatting codes that specify text display colors, and you can create *conditional formats*, which only use a specific format when the value being displayed meets a certain criteria.

This is best seen by looking at one of the predefined formats within Excel. The following is one of the predefined formats within the Currency category:

$#,##0.00_);[RED]($#,##0.00)

Notice that there are two formats, divided by a semicolon. If there are two formats like this, Excel assumes that the one on the left is to be used if the number is 0 or above, and the one on the right is to be used if the number is less than 0. This example results in all numbers having a dollar sign, a comma being used as a thousands separator, amounts less than $1.00 having a leading 0, and negative values being shown in red with surrounding parentheses. The _) part of the left format is used so that positive and negative numbers align properly (positive numbers will leave a space, the same width as a right parentheses) after the number).

Using conditionals and colors, you can get very complex in your formats. For instance, let's assume you were formatting a telephone number, and you used the following formatting codes:

[>9999999](000) 000-0000;[<0][RED]"Phone Number Error";000-0000

This results in a correctly formatting phone number, no matter what. If there is an area code, it is shown in parentheses; if a negative number is in the cell, then an error message is displayed; otherwise, the phone number is shown as seven digits with the dash in the proper place.

You can experiment with conditionals and colors to devise the best displays for your data. Table 14.5 shows the color and conditional formatting codes. As you can tell from the examples already provided, these codes are used with those already discussed in the previous two sections.

Symbol	Meaning
[BLACK]	Display information with black type
[BLUE]	Display information with blue type
[CYAN]	Display information with cyan type
[GREEN]	Display information with green type
[MAGENTA]	Display information with magenta type
[RED]	Display information with red type

Table 14.5 Excel condition and color number-formatting codes. (continued on next page)

Symbol	Meaning
[WHITE]	Display information with white type
[YELLOW]	Display information with yellow type
[COLOR *x*]	Display information with type with the color code *x*, where *x* can be any value from 1 to 64
[= *value*]	Use this format only if the number equals this *value*
[< *value*]	Use this format only if the number is less than this *value*
[<= *value*]	Use this format only if the number is less than or equals this *value*
[> *value*]	Use this format only if the number is greater than this *value*
[>= *value*]	Use this format only if the number is greater than or equals this *value*
[<> *value*]	Use this format only if the number does not equal this *value*

Table 14.5 Excel condition and color number-formatting codes. (continued from previous page)

USING FRACTIONAL NUMBER FORMATS

In some industries, fractions are the norm. For instance, the building industry routinely uses fractions to measure lumber and distances. One of the unique features of excel is that it allows you to use fractional numbers. For instance, you can enter a number as 12.25 and have it displayed as 12 1/4.

The predefined number formats have a few formats provided in the Fraction category, however there is a good chance that these will not meet your needs. When you define your own fraction formats, Excel assumes that if you provide digit placeholders on both sides of the slash (/), you are defining a fractional format. For instance, if you are working with inches, you can define the following format:

```
#–#/##\"
```

This results in numbers such as 18.75 being displayed as 18–3/4". This is exactly what the building contractor may need to convey specifications or other measurements.

When you define fractional formats, make sure that you use, as the denominator to the fraction, the maximum number of digits you want to appear there. In the above example, the largest fraction that can be displayed is 98/99. If you want larger denominators, you must explicitly format for them, as in:

        #–#/###\"

WHAT YOU NEED TO KNOW

Excel allows you to format your numbers in any way you desire. The predefined formats and the built-in formatting codes provide a power and flexibility that you can't find in other spreadsheet programs.

While the formatting codes provided in this lesson might appear confusing, there is a good chance that you will never need to use them. It is good to know, however, that Excel can provide the capabilities you need in case you find later that you must use them. In this lesson you have learned the following major items:

- ☑ Internally, Excel tracks numbers up to 15 digits of precision. Externally, you have complete control over how you want Excel to display numbers.

- ☑ Excel is provided with a wide array of predefined number formats that can be selected from the Number file card (visible when you select Cell from the Format menu).

- ☑ You can use several of the tools on the formatting toolbar to quickly apply formats to numbers.

- ☑ If you have needs beyond the number formats provided with Excel, you can create your own custom formats. Excel provides a complete and powerful formatting capability that is at your disposal.

- ☑ Unlike many spreadsheet programs, Excel allows you to display numbers in a fractional format.

In the next lesson you will learn how to change further the way in which information is displayed in cells. You will learn about alignment and fonts.

Lesson 15

Changing How Cells Look

The building blocks of Excel are cells. While it can be argued that rows and columns make up your sheets, these are nothing but collections of cells. Understanding how to control how cells look is fundamental to the design and layout of your sheets.

Formatting cells involves three main topics—the cell itself (color and patterns), the cell alignment, and the text within the cell (font and color). In this lesson you will start with the basics to learn about fonts and progress to cells and alignment. By learning how you can change the looks of your cells, you learn how to change the look of your entire sheet. You will learn

- What fonts are
- How to change fonts
- How to change cell colors and patterns
- How to change font colors
- How to change cell alignment
- About adding borders to cells

CHANGING FONT INFORMATION

Excel allows you complete control over how text and numbers appear within your workbook. You can change either individual selections of text within a cell, or you can change all the text within large ranges of cells. The following sections teach you how you can control every aspect of the fonts within your workbook.

WHAT IS A FONT?

In simple terms, a *font* represents a certain way of printing letters, numbers, and other symbols. These fonts are given names that are either dictated by tradition or that loosely represent the appearance of the font. For instance, Courier is a common font, as is Helvetica and Times Roman. There are literally thousands of fonts on the market today, each being sold by different vendors. Excel supports any font that you can load into Windows, including bitmapped, Adobe, and TrueType fonts.

Fonts are measured in *points*. A point is roughly equivalent to 1/72 of an inch. Thus, a 10-point typeface has characters that are roughly 10/72 of an inch in height. Later in this lesson you will learn how to change the height of a font within Excel; all such changes are done using points.

In general, there are four types of fonts. These are

- Serif fonts
- Sans serif fonts
- Symbol fonts
- Decorative fonts

Serif fonts are those that have embellishments on the letters which make them appear more pleasing and less angular. For example, the font used in this book is a serif font. Notice the serifs on the following New Century Schoolbook type sample:

Serifs —————<This has serifs

A *sans serif* font (meaning, literally, *without serif*) does not have the flourishes on the strokes of each letter. For instance, the following is in Helvetica, a common sans serif font:

This has no serifs

While sans serif is fine for shorter lines of text such as headings, a serif font is better suited for longer lines and text that will probably be read for longer periods of time.

Symbol fonts are used to display graphics symbols. There are many different types of symbol fonts, for example Symbol, Wingdings, and ZapfDingbats. These fonts might include characters such as the following:

Finally, *decorative fonts* are used primarily for titles, headings, and special flourishes. They are not good for general text, as they are typically large, bold, and designed to stand out from other typefaces around them. Examples include Cooper, Billboard, Ink Pad, Cargo, or ZapfChancery. The following is an example using the ZapfChancery typeface:

This is a decorative font

CONTROLLING THE FONT

If you want to change a fonts within Excel, you must first select the cells or the text you want to format. This is done as was described in Lesson 6, "Entering and Changing Information." If you are formatting entire cells, it's not important that the cells have anything in them; you can format the cells before they actually contain information. When you later add the information, it will assume the format you last set, including the font.

Once the cells or text are selected, you can change the font by clicking on the arrow next to the font field on the formatting toolbar. When you do, you will see a list of fonts will drop down, from which you can choose one:

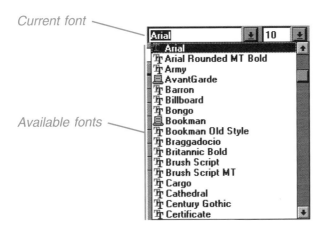

You can scroll through the available fonts the same way you scroll through many other options within Excel. When you select a font, the change is made immediately.

APPLYING TEXT ATTRIBUTES

Text attributes can be viewed as nothing more than modifications to the base font. For instance, you may use the bold attribute to emphasize your text, or italics might be used to indicate a quote. Excel refers to these text attributes as *font styles*. Common text attributes can be easily applied with the buttons on the formatting toolbar. There are three text attribute buttons provided, as listed in Table 15.1.

Button	Meaning
B	Bold
I	Italics
U	Underlined

Table 15.1 Text-attribute formatting buttons available on the toolbar.

There are other types of underlines available in Excel, but these cannot be applied from the formatting toolbar. Instead you must use the full cell formatting features of Excel. This is done by using the menus, as described later in this lesson.

CHANGING POINT SIZES

Earlier in this lesson you learned that font sizes are specified in points. This is a typographer's measure that is equal to approximately 1/72 of an inch. To change the point size of a text selection, you can use the formatting toolbar. Just to the left of the text attribute buttons is the point size field. If you click on the arrow to the right of this field, you are presented with a list of point sizes you can choose:

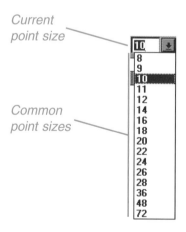

Current point size

Common point sizes

Excel allows you to specify any font size between 1 and 409 points. (This depends, of course, on the capabilities of your printer.) To pick a point size, simply scroll through the list and choose the one you want. Click on the point size, and your text is updated. You can also type one in from the keyboard

As it stores your workbook on disk, Excel keeps track of point sizes (along with other text-formatting information). You can, if you desire, change the point size of every letter in your workbook. While such a creation might be difficult to read, it is certainly not beyond the capabilities of Excel.

Changing Font Color

The formatting toolbar provides a quick way you can change the color of the font you are using. This is done with the ▣ tool. This tool actually has two parts. If you click on the ▣ part, the color shown in the small square is applied to whatever you have selected. If you click on the arrow at the right side of the tool, you will see a color palette appear:

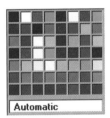

To select a color, click on one of the small color squares. This color is applied to your selection, and appears in the small square on the font color tool. If you don't have a color printer, don't worry—you can still use the color to highlight text on the screen, and Excel will print the text in black and white as if the colors had not been changed at all.

Changing Font Information All At Once

So far in this lesson you have learned how to modify font information from the formatting toolbar. While there are many tasks you can perform with the formatting toolbar, there are some that are best left to the Cells option of the Format menu. When you choose this option, you will see the Format Cells dialog box, as shown in Figure 15.1; make sure you have the Font file card selected:

Font
file card

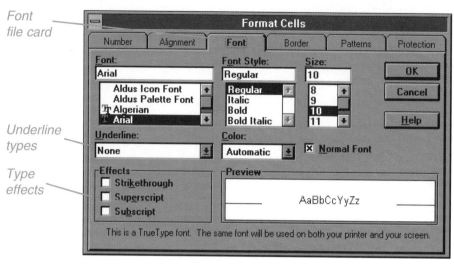

Underline
types

Type
effects

Figure 15.1 The Format Cells dialog box showing the Font file card.

Based on earlier discussions, many of the fields in this dialog box should already look familiar. Notice, however, that there are several settings that are not available from the formatting toolbar. These include the different underline types and the type effects (lower- left corner).

As you make any changes to the character formatting, you can see the effect in the sample text shown in the dialog box. When you are satisfied with the formatting you have applied, click on the
OK button.

CHANGING CELL ATTRIBUTES

Now that you have learned how you can control how fonts appear, you need to learn about formatting the cell itself. Excel allows you to control three different cell-formatting attributes—cell alignment, color, and patterns. These are each discussed in the next few sections.

CHANGING CELL ALIGNMENT

There are two ways you can align cell information in Excel. The first (and easiest) is to use the alignment buttons on the formatting toolbar. When you click on one of these buttons, any cells you have selected are aligned in that way. There are four of these buttons, shown in Table 15.2.

Button	Meaning
	Left alignment
	Center alignment
	Right alignment
	Centered across selected cells

Table 15.2 Cell alignment buttons available on the formatting toolbar.

The first three alignment buttons should be fairly self explanatory; they function much as alignment commands do in your word processor. The last alignment button might need a bit of explaining, however. Before choosing this button, make sure that the text you want to align is in the first cell of a horizontal range of cells. Then click on ⊞, and the text is centered, not within the cell boundaries, but across the entire range you selected. This is great for putting headings on sheets where each column is a different width.

The other method for setting cell alignment is to use the Cells option from the Format menu. When you choose this option, make sure you have the Alignment file card selected, and you will see the Format Cells dialog box, as shown in Figure 15.2; make sure the Alignment file card is displayed.

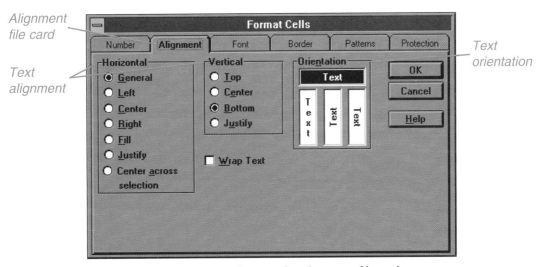

Figure 15.2 The Format Cells dialog box showing the Alignment file card.

Some of the options in the dialog box should already look familiar (they are available from the formatting toolbar). Other options, however, are available only from this dialog box. For instance, Excel allows you to control vertical alignment within the cell and to change orientation of the text in a cell. If you decide to change the alignment, Excel automatically adjusts the row height so that the text fits within the row.

After you have specified how you want information to appear within the cell, you can click on OK to accomplish the choice.

CHANGING CELL COLOR

Earlier in this lesson you learned how you can change the font color. Excel also lets you change the color used to fill the entire cell. This, again, can be done either from the formatting toolbar or a dialog box.

To change cell color from the formatting toolbar, use the tool. This tool actually has two parts. If you click on the part, then the color shown in the small square is applied to the cells you have selected. Note that the color of the text doesn't change, only the color of the cell background.

If you click on the arrow at the right side of the tool, you will see a color palette appear:

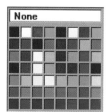

To select a color, click on one of the small color squares. This color is applied to the cells you have selected, and appears in the small square on the cell color tool.

The other method of changing cell color is to choose the Cells option from the Format menu. You will see the Format Cells dialog box, as shown in Figure 15.3; make sure you have the Patterns file card selected:

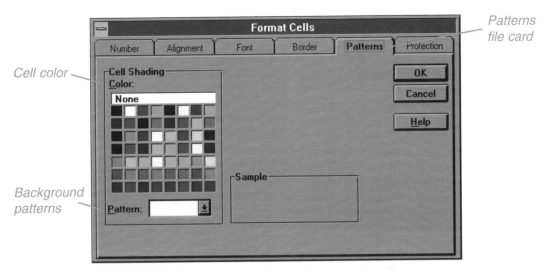

Patterns file card

Cell color

Background patterns

Figure 15.3 The Format Cells dialog box showing the Patterns file card.

Notice that this dialog box contains the same color palette shown when you click on the right side of the cell color button on the formatting toolbar. You can select a color, and then click on OK to make the change.

If you don't have a color printer, make sure you select light colors for the cell background. Excel will always try to approximate colors for the printer you have, and dark colors will print dark, perhaps obscuring the print in the cell. Therefore, light colors are best when you don't have a color output device.

Another thing to watch is that you don't choose the same text and background color. If you do, your cells will appear empty, when in fact they aren't. To remedy this, simply change either the cell or text color so they are different.

CHANGING CELL PATTERNS

Besides changing colors used in cells, Excel also allows you to change the background pattern used in the cell. To do this, choose Cells from the Format menu, and make sure you have the Patterns file card selected. You will see the Format Cells dialog box, as shown earlier. If you click on the arrow to the right of the Patterns field, you will see a list of 18 patterns and a color palette, which you can use:

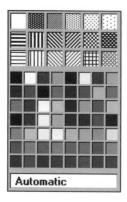

Select a pattern and then select a color you want used for the marks used to create the pattern. By creatively combining patterns, pattern colors, and cell background colors, you can create hundreds (if not thousands) of special effects.

ADDING A BORDER

Another formatting feature which Excel allows you to use is borders. You can add borders around one or a group of cells. This is done by first selecting the cell or cells you wish to border, and then selecting the Cells option from the Format menu. You will see the Format Cells dialog box, as shown in Figure 15.4; make sure that the Borders file card is selected:

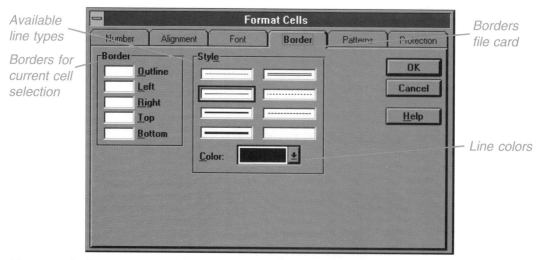

Figure 15.4 The Format Cells dialog box showing the Borders file card.

Adding the border is as simple as selecting one of the eight line types from the right side of the dialog box, and then (in the Borders area) clicking on the side of the cell selection you want the line applied. If you click the Outline option, the cell selection is outlined with the line type you have selected. When you then click on [**OK**], the border is added to the selected cells.

WHAT YOU NEED TO KNOW

Excel provides complete control over how information is displayed in a cell. You can change the font, font attributes, font colors, cell alignment, cell colors, and cell patterns. In this lesson you have learned how you can exercise this control. In particular, you have learned

- ☑ Fonts are nothing but a pattern of how letters, numbers, and special symbols should appear when printed.

- ☑ Excel allows you to change the fonts used to display information in your sheet. You can change the font, its size and style, or its color.

- ☑ Alignment refers to how information within a cell is positioned in relation to the cell itself. Excel allows you complete control over both horizontal and vertical alignment.

- ☑ Besides changing the color of information within a cell, Excel allows you to change the color of the cell itself. You can also modify the pattern used to fill the cell and change the color used to draw the pattern.

- ☑ Borders can be easily added to cells to highlight any information you desire.

In the next lesson you will learn how to expand your control over rows and columns.

Lesson 16

Working with Rows and Columns

In Lesson 15 you learned that Excel allows you complete control over the way in which information appears within cells. In this lesson you will learn how you can work with the most common groupings of cells: rows and columns. By the end of this lesson you will have learned the following:

- How to adjust row height

- How to control the display of rows

- How to adjust column width

- How to set the standard column width

- How to control the display of columns

- What AutoFit means

Adjusting Row Height

As far as Excel is concerned, row height is a rather dynamic thing. It is determined by the height of the largest font on each line, multiplied by the number of text lines in the row. This is calculated for each cell in the row, and the largest value becomes the row height for the entire row.

There may be times, however, when you want to adjust the row height manually. This is done in either of two ways. The first way is to use the mouse, while the second involves use of the menus.

To use the mouse to adjust row height, move the mouse pointer into the row headers at the left side of your sheet. As you position the pointer over the dividing line between two rows, notice that it changes to a double-headed arrow:

Row height adjustment cursor

When the mouse pointer looks like this, you can adjust the row height of the row just above the pointer (in this example, row 6) by dragging it. Click and hold the left mouse button. As you move the mouse, the row height adjusts, as well. When you release the mouse button, that is the height the row will retain.

You can adjust the height of more than one row at a time by first selecting the rows whose height you want to adjust (click on the row headers so the entire rows are selected), and then adjusting the height of any row in the selection. When you release the mouse button, the height of all rows in the selection will be changed to that same height. You can also use the menus to adjust row height. This is done by selecting the Row option from the Format menu. When you do, you will see a submenu:

Select the **Height** option and you will see the Row Height dialog box, as shown in Figure 16.1:

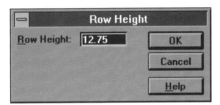

Figure 16.1 The Row Height dialog box.

Enter a value representing the desired row height, in points. The default value shown is the current row height. When you click on ▄ **OK** ▄, the row height is changed.

HIDING AND UNHIDING ROWS

There may be times when you want to hide a row completely from view. While this can be done by using the mouse to shrink the height of the row to nothing (covered in the previous section), this is not the easiest way. The easiest way is to choose the Row option from the Format menu. Then, from the submenu that is displayed, select Hide. This sets the height of the selected rows to 0, effectively hiding them.

Note: When you hide rows, Excel can still access them. Any formulas that rely on information in the hidden row will still work properly. Excel also does not renumber the rows that are left displayed. Thus, if you hide row 7, the row headers skip directly from 6 to 8. This is the way you can tell whether there are any hidden rows.

If you later want to unhide the rows, you can do so using the menus by selecting the rows on both sides of the hidden row. If, for example, row 7 is hidden and you want to unhide it, you can select rows 6 and 8, choose the Row option from the Format menu, and click on Unhide. The hidden row reappears, set to the height it was before you first hid it.

You can also use the mouse to unhide rows, although this method does not retain the original row height. To use the mouse to unhide rows, move the mouse pointer into the row header area, positioning it just below the thick line that denotes the hidden row (or rows). Notice that the mouse pointer changes to a double-headed arrow, but it is different than the arrow used to adjust regular row height:

Reveal hidden row cursor

Click and hold down the left mouse button. Drag the mouse downward; when you release the mouse button, the hidden row will reappear and be set to that height. If more than one row was hidden, only the last of the hidden rows will appear. If you want to unhide more than one row at a time, you must use the menu method previously introduced.

ADJUSTING COLUMN WIDTH

Column width is adjusted in much the same manner as adjusting row height. As with rows, you can use either the mouse or the menus to adjust the column width. To use the mouse, move the mouse pointer into the column header area. As you move the pointer over a dividing line between columns, it changes to a double-headed arrow:

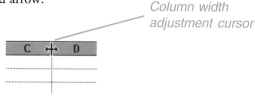

Column width adjustment cursor

When the mouse pointer looks like this, you can adjust the column width of the column to the left of the pointer (in this example, column C). Click and hold the left mouse button. As you move the mouse, the column width adjusts, as well. When you release the mouse button, the width the column will stay at that width.

Note: Make sure you grab the column headers, selecting entire columns, rather than merely highlighting several cells in the same row. If something unexpected occurs when you try this operation, that might be the reason.

You can adjust the width of more than one column at a time by first selecting the columns and then adjusting the width of any column in the selection. When you release the mouse button, the width of all columns in the selection will be changed to that same width.

You can also use the menus to adjust column width. To do this, select the Column option from the Format menu. When you do, you will see a submenu:

Select the Width option and you will see the Column Width dialog box, as shown in Figure 16.2:

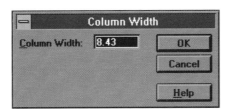

Figure 16.2 The Column Width dialog box.

Enter a value representing the desired column width. This number represents the number of characters that can be displayed in a cell for the current font and size. The value shown is the width of the column selected. When you click on OK, the column width is changed.

SETTING THE STANDARD COLUMN WIDTH

Unlike the row height (where there is no set standard), Excel maintains a standard column width. This width is used as a default when you have not explicitly defined how wide you want a column to be. To set the standard column width (or see what it currently is), choose Column from the Format menu and choose Standard Width from the submenu. You will see the Standard Width dialog box, as shown in Figure 16.3:

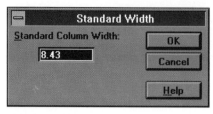

Figure 16.3 *The Standard Width dialog box.*

Here you can enter a new value that will be used for all columns in your sheet (except those you have explicitly set the width on). When you click on 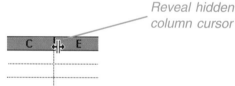, the display is updated to reflect the new standard column width.

Excel also lets you set the width of any other column back to the standard width by selecting the columns you want to reset before you choose the Standard Width command.

HIDING AND UNHIDING COLUMNS

Hiding and unhiding columns via the menus is done in the same manner as hiding and unhiding rows. The only difference is that you choose Hide and Unhide from the Columns submenu.

Using the mouse is similar, as well. All you need to do is move the mouse pointer into the column header area. As you move the pointer over a thick divider that indicates a hidden column (or columns), it changes to this:

Reveal hidden column cursor

Don't confuse this with the pointer used to adjust the column width. Notice that there is a split opening between the double arrows. Click and hold the left mouse button as you move the mouse to the right. When you release the mouse button, the hidden column is displayed and has the width that you set. If more than one column was hidden, only the rightmost hidden column will appear. If you want to unhide more than one column at a time, you must use the menu method.

UNDERSTANDING AUTOFIT

You probably notice that both the Row and Column submenus have an AutoFit option. In the Column submenu it is called AutoFit Selection, while in the Row submenu it is simply called AutoFit. There is a difference between these two choices. When working on rows, AutoFit sets the row height back to a default. This means that the row height will be equal to the cell containing the most lines multiplied by the size of the largest font (the same as described at the first of this lesson).

If you use AutoFit on a column, Excel sets the column width wide enough to display the text in the selected cell. AutoFit can also be used by double-clicking on the right side of the column header for that column. The column width is adjusted to reflect the width of the widest text in the column.

WHAT YOU NEED TO KNOW

Excel gives you a great deal of flexibility in how you display rows and columns. You can adjust the height and width to reflect the data you are displaying, or simply according to your personal preference. In this lesson you have learned the following:

- ☑ Excel uses a default row height based on the size of the font used to display the cell information. You can override this default and set the row height to any size desired.

- ☑ Rows can be hidden completely, thereby preventing them from being either seen or printed. This has no effect on formulas within the sheet.

- ☑ When you first open a workbook, Excel sets the width of each column to a default value. It is not uncommon to adjust the column width to better display information within the column.

- ☑ If you find yourself adjusting the widths of many different columns, you can change the default column width in order to affect entire sheets.

- ☑ If desired, columns can be hidden from view and from printing. This has no effect on formulas within the sheet.

- ☑ The AutoFit feature can be used to automatically adjust the size of either rows or columns.

The next lesson will cover a larger issue: adjusting what your entire sheet and workbook looks like.

Lesson 17

Changing How Workbooks Look

So far in this section you have learned how to format numbers and cells, and modify rows and columns. There is still one level of formatting left to discuss—your individual sheets and entire workbooks. This lesson covers this area of formatting, focusing on how to make your sheets look their best on the printed page. You will learn:

- How to adjust page settings

- What scaling is and how to use it

- How to adjust margins

- How to set page headers and footers

- How to control what prints

ADJUSTING PAGE SETTINGS

Perhaps the first thing to do when you are formatting your pages is to specify your *page size* and *page orientation.* This means you need to specify the dimensions of the paper you will be using, as well as how your text prints in relation to the page. Both tasks are accomplished by selecting Page Setup from the File menu. When you do, you will see the Page Setup dialog box, as shown in Figure 17.1; make sure you select the Page file card:

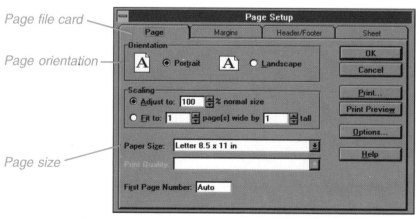

Figure 17.1 The Page Setup dialog box showing the Page file card.

In Excel, *page size* refers to the physical size of the paper on which you will print your sheet. In most cases, this will be a standard size, such as letter size or legal size. In many cases, the limits on your page size are determined by your printer.

To set the page size, click on the arrow to the right of the Paper Size field. When you do, you will see a drop-down list that indicates the paper sizes that Excel supports for your printer. The most common sizes are shown in Table 17.1.

Size	Dimensions
Letter	8.5" × 11"
Legal	8.5" × 14"
A4	210 mm × 297 mm
B5	182 mm × 257 mm

Table 17.1 Common paper sizes supported by Excel.

Once you have specified the size of your paper, you can specify the *page orientation*. This represents how Excel should position the type in relation to the page. There are two different page orientations: *portrait* and *landscape*. Portrait orientation is where the paper is taller than it is wide; landscape orientation is the opposite.

To set orientation, locate the box labeled Orientation in the Page Setup dialog box. The two buttons in this box determine whether Excel will use portrait or landscape orientation. Click on the appropriate button.

When you have finished setting the page size and orientation, you can click on the OK button.

UNDERSTANDING SCALING

Take another look at the Page file card of the Page Setup dialog box, as shown in Figure 17.1. You will notice that in the center of the dialog box there is an area entitled Scaling. Page scaling is a big boon over printing in earlier versions of Excel. With page scaling you have two options. First, you can directly scale your output by specifying how much to enlarge or shrink the image that is printed. Excel allows you to set scaling at any value between 10 percent and 400 percent of normal size. If you are using a PostScript printer, this works wonderfully. Results on other printers will depend on the quality and capabilities of the printer.

The second option is closely related to direct scaling, but approaches it in a much more functional manner. If you enable the **Fit to** option, you can indicate how many pages you want the final output to be. You should understand that this option will not enlarge the output, but is designed to shrink it to meet a specific page requirement. Thus, if you need your output to fit on a single page, you can specify that the output be one page wide and one page tall.

*Note: One of the tricks I use is to set the **Fit to** settings to one page wide by 99 pages tall. In this way, I am sure that the output will fit on one page across, but then Excel controls how many pages long the document will be.*

SETTING PAGE MARGINS

In Excel, page margins are used to determine how much white space (blank area) should be left around your text. Margins are used to provide a visual border for your printed page, and they provide an area where the page can be held or bound.

To set margins, choose the Page Setup option from the File menu, as shown in Figure 17.2. Make sure that the Margins file card is selected:

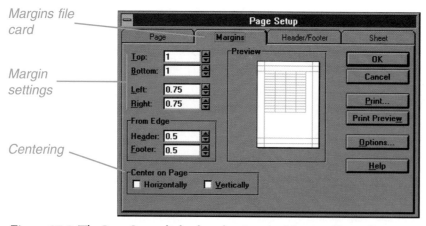

Margins file card

Margin settings

Centering

Figure 17.2 The Page Setup dialog box showing the Margins file card.

Notice that there are four margins you can specify: top, bottom, left, and right. Each margin refers to the distance from the edge of the paper to where the sheet is printed. Thus, a one-inch top margin means that there will be one inch of white space at the top of each page of your document. You should note, however, that headers and footers (discussed later in this lesson) can be printed within the top and bottom margins.

At the bottom of the dialog box there are some check boxes that control the centering of your information on the page. Clicking on either the Horizontally or Vertically check boxes will make sure that your information is centered in that direction. Notice that as you make changes to the margins or to the information centering, Excel shows you what your layout looks like. This is shown in the Preview area in the center of the dialog box. When you have finished making changes, click on the OK button.

SETTING PAGE HEADERS AND FOOTERS

Headers and footers appear at the top and bottom of each page in your printout. As an example, this book uses headers and footers. The *header*, at the top of the page, indicates the book or lesson name, while the *footer*, at the bottom of the page, includes just the page number. You can include similar headers and footers when you print your workbook.

In the previous section you learned how you can set the location of the header and footer. This section focuses on actually defining what appears in the header and footer. To work with headers and footers, you should select the Page Setup option from the File menu, making sure the Header/Footer file card is selected. You will see the Page Setup dialog box, as shown in Figure 17.3:

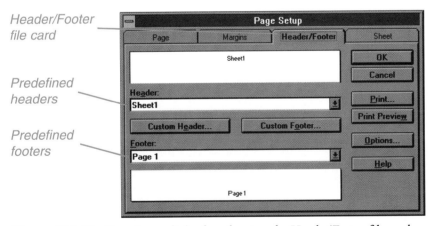

Figure 17.3 The Page Setup dialog box showing the Header/Footer file card.

Setting your headers and footers is done in the same manner. To select a predefined header, all you need to do is click on the arrow to the right of the Header or Footer fields and choose one of them. If none of these are the way you want them, you can create a new header or footer by clicking on the Custom Header... or Custom Footer... buttons.

Suppose, for example, that you want to create a new header. When you click on the ![Custom Header...] button, you will see the dialog box shown in Figure 17.4:

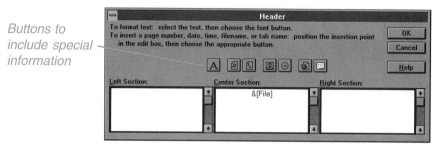

Buttons to include special information

Figure 17.4 *The Header dialog box.*

Here you can define what you want on the left, center, and right portions of the header. When you have finished, click on [OK], and the newly defined header is added to the list of predefined headers. Click on [OK] again, and the headers and footers are set for your sheet.

CONTROLLING WHAT PRINTS

There is one other area of workbook and sheet formatting that is used to control what is sent to the printer. For instance, you can control which area of the sheet is printed, whether any titles are repeated on each page of the printout, what is included with the printout, and the order in which the pages are printed. To modify these settings, choose Page Setup from the File menu, and make sure the Sheet file card is selected. The Page Setup dialog box will appear as shown in Figure 17.5:

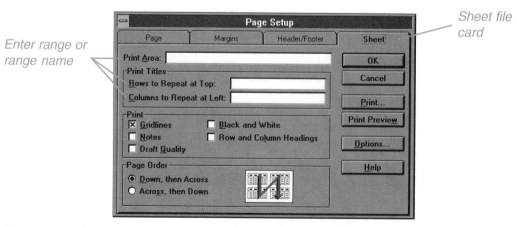

Sheet file card

Enter range or range name

Figure 17.5 *The Page Setup dialog box showing the Sheet file card.*

The three fields at the top of the dialog box (Print Area and those in the Print Titles box) are used to hold ranges of cells. In the Print Area field you can enter either an actual range (such as A10:F42) or a name which has been assigned to a range (see Lesson 9). Similarly, you can enter a number of rows or columns in the Print Titles area. This number of rows or columns will be printed on every page of your printout.

The settings in the Print area are the ones you will most likely change. These settings control how the information in your sheet is printed. You can set the following items:

Option	Function
Gridlines	If selected, the gridlines which display on the screen will also appear on the printout.
Notes	If selected, any notes you have attached to cells will also print.
Draft Quality	If selected, a draft version of the sheet is printed. Graphics will not print and fonts will not match exactly those that were specified. This is a good way to see a proof of a sheet before a final print is made.
Black and White	If selected, don't try to print in color; approximate all colors to black and white.
Row and Column Headings	If selected, then the row and column headings which appear on the screen will also appear on the printout.

Table 17.2 Print options in the Sheet file card of the Page Setup dialog box.

Finally, in the area at the bottom of the dialog box you can specify the order in which you want Excel to print pages. If you have more data than will fit on a single page, then this option allows you to indicate whether Excel should print from top to bottom and then left to right, or the opposite. Make your selection based on how you want the pages ordered.

When you have finished specifying how you want your sheet to print, click on `OK`.

QUICK REVIEW

Excel allows you to control how your workbooks look when they are printed. You can adjust page margins, headers, footers, scaling, and other options by choosing the Page Setup from the File menu. This displays the Page Setup dialog box, which allows you to change the workbook printing settings.

What You Need to Know

You already know that Excel is a powerful spreadsheet program. No less powerful is the ability Excel provides to control how your information is printed. In this lesson you have learned the formatting techniques you can apply to adjust your page layout for the best possible printing. Specifically, you have learned the following:

- ☑ By choosing the Page Setup option from the File menu, Excel allows you to control settings which directly affect how a page appears when printed.

- ☑ Excel provides automatic scaling that, if used, can adjust the size of the entire sheet so it will print within a certain number of pages.

- ☑ Within Excel, page margins—the white space left at the edges of a printed page—can be adjusted to any desired size.

- ☑ You can define what Excel prints in the top and bottom margins of each page of your sheet. These are called headers (at the top) and footers (at the bottom).

- ☑ Excel allows you to control the portions of your sheet which are actually printed.

In the next section you will learn about the tremendous power and convenience provided by styles: how to create, apply, change, merge, save and delete them.

Lesson 18

Using Styles

By this point you should be fairly comfortable with using Excel. You know how to enter, edit, and save text. You also know how to format your sheets and print your workbooks. In this lesson you will learn about styles, a form of "formatting shorthand" employed by Excel. This lesson teaches you how to

- Create styles

- Use styles in your workbook

- Make changes to existing styles

- Merge styles from other workbooks

- Save styles

- Delete styles

CREATING STYLES

A *style* is nothing more than a pattern for how you want a cell to look. In Lesson 15 you learned how you can change the appearance of cells; styles save that formatting under a user-defined name so you can later apply it to other cells in your sheet.

For example, suppose you use headings frequently in your sheet (perhaps to divide sections of your sheet). If you wanted the heading to be in 15-point Garamond font, boldface, italic, and blue, you could perform each of these formatting tasks, one by one, each time you enter such a head, or you could define a style (perhaps named Heading) that performs all of these formatting tasks with the click of a button.

The easiest way to define a style is to first format the cell as you want it to appear. Make all your changes to the font, number format, alignment, color, patterns, and borders that you want. When it appears as you want it to, choose the Style option from the Format menu. You will then see the Style dialog box, as shown in Figure 18.1:

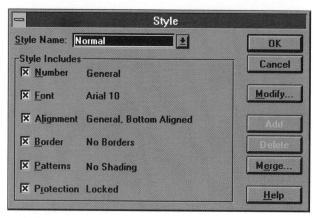

Figure 18.1 The Style dialog box.

In the Style Name field, enter the name you want this style to be known by. When you type the name of the style (if it is not already defined), notice that just under the Style Name field Excel puts a message:

This indicates that Excel assumes you are creating a style based on the format in the current cell. Once the name is entered, all you need to do is click on the [Add] button, and the style is retained by Excel.

You can also define a style that is not based on the current cell, even though Excel always assumes you will be doing so. This is done by entering the style name, and then clicking on the [Modify...] button. You will then see the Format Cell dialog box, as covered in Lesson 15. When you exit that dialog box, you return to the Style dialog box where you can add the style by clicking on [Add]

APPLYING STYLES

Once you have defined styles, you can apply them throughout your sheet as you deem appropriate. Make sure you select the cell or cells you want to format with the style. Then select Style from the Format menu, and you will see the Style dialog box (shown earlier in Figure 18.1).

Click on the arrow to the right of the Style Name field, and you will see a list of defined styles, as shown in Figure 18.2:

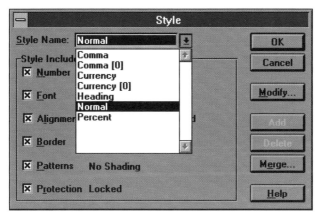

Figure 18.2 *The Style dialog box showing the Style Name list pulled down.*

In the Styles list, select the style you want to use. Then click on the OK button. The attributes for that style are then applied to the selected cells.

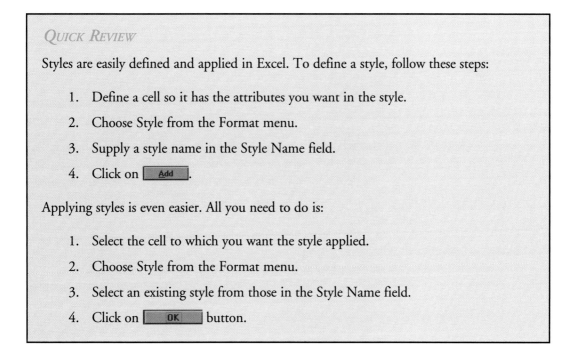

QUICK REVIEW

Styles are easily defined and applied in Excel. To define a style, follow these steps:

1. Define a cell so it has the attributes you want in the style.

2. Choose Style from the Format menu.

3. Supply a style name in the Style Name field.

4. Click on Add.

Applying styles is even easier. All you need to do is:

1. Select the cell to which you want the style applied.

2. Choose Style from the Format menu.

3. Select an existing style from those in the Style Name field.

4. Click on OK button.

ADVANTAGES OF STYLES

The largest single advantage of styles is that you only have to define a format once, and then it can be applied throughout your sheet. For instance, if you are using the predefined style called Normal, and you later decide that you want these types of cells to be use a different font, all you need to do is change the style. After changing the style, every cell in your sheet that is formatted with the Normal style is changed to the new font. This is done automatically; there is nothing else that needs to be done on your part.

CHANGING EXISTING STYLES

Styles within Excel can be easily changed at any time. This is done by choosing the Style option from the Format menu. You will then see the Style dialog box, shown earlier. To change an existing style:

1. Select, within the Styles list, the style you want to change.

2. Click on [Modify...]. You will see the Format Cell dialog box, described fully in Lesson 15.

3. Make the formatting changes as desired.

4. Click on the [OK] button. You will return to the Style dialog box.

Repeat these steps for each style you wish to modify. When you have finished, click on the [OK] button.

MERGING STYLES

Merging is the term Excel uses to describe the process of copying styles from one workbook to another. For instance, suppose you want to use the styles defined in your SALES.XLS workbook in a new workbook you are creating. You can copy the styles from SALES.XLS. When you do, the styles in SALES.XLS will be copied to the new book and will replace any styles in the new workbook that happen to have the same name.

To copy styles, open both workbooks (the one you want to copy from and the one you want to copy to). Make sure that the workbook you want to copy to is the active workbook, then choose Style from the Format menu. You will see the Style dialog box, shown earlier. Click on the [Merge...] button. You will then see the Merge Styles dialog box, as shown in Figure 18.3:

List of other
open workbooks

Figure 18.3 *The Merge Styles dialog box.*

From the list of workbooks, choose the one from which you want to copy styles and click on OK. Excel will display the dialog box, shown in Figure 18.4, asking you to confirm what you are doing. Click on OK, and the merge will be complete.

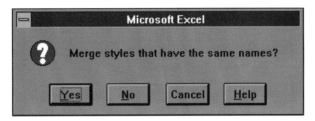

Figure 18.4 *Click Yes to merge styles.*

SAVING STYLES

There is very little you need to do to save styles. In fact, there are only two requirements. The first is to make sure you click on the OK button instead of the Cancel button in the Style dialog box. The second is to simply save your workbook. Styles are automatically saved with the workbook on which you are working.

DELETING STYLES

After you have been working with a workbook for some time, you might reach a point when you want to delete some styles. This is easy to do, using the same Style dialog box as used with the other style-related procedures described in this lesson.

To delete a style, follow these steps:

1. Choose Style from the Format menu. You will see the Style dialog box, shown earlier.

2. Click on the arrow to the right of the Style Name field. You will see a list of the available styles.

3. Choose the style you want to delete.

4. Click on the [**Delete**] button.

Repeat steps 2 through 4 for any other styles you want to delete. When you have finished, click on the [**OK**] button.

WHAT YOU NEED TO KNOW

If you find yourself making elaborate spreadsheets that use quite a few of the same formats over and over again, you would be wise to investigate styles. Excel allows you to use styles to save time and energy. The other advantage is that they cut down on formatting errors. In this lesson you have learned:

- ☑ Styles provide a pattern you can use to format similar information in different parts of your sheet.

- ☑ You can add styles by selecting the Style option from the Format menu. Once you have set the formatting information as you want it, you only need to click on the [**Add**] button.

- ☑ To apply a style, select the cell or cell range you want formatted, and then choose the Style option from the Format menu. From the list of available styles, choose the one desired and then click on the [**OK**] button.

- ☑ Once a style is defined, it is not defined forever. Excel also allows you to change styles, copy them between workbooks, and delete them.

- ☑ When you save your workbook, the styles you have defined are saved with the other spreadsheet information.

In the next lesson you will learn how to copy formats, from one cell to another and from one cell to many.

Lesson 19

Copying Formatting

In Lesson 18 you learned about a styles, a formatting shortcut you can use to speed up formatting of your workbook. In this lesson you will learn of another shortcut—copying formatting from one cell to another. You will learn:

- How to copy formatting once with the Format Painter
- How to copy formatting many times with the Format Painter
- How to paste formats
- Which formats are copied

USING THE FORMAT PAINTER

As you already know, the vast majority of formatting tools are available on the formatting toolbar. There is one formatting tool available on the standard toolbar, however. This is the Format Painter (⬚). Using this tool, you can quickly copy formatting from one location in your workbook to another. The way you use this tool depends on the type of formatting you wish to perform.

COPYING FROM ONE CELL TO ANOTHER

The quickest way to use the Format Painter is to copy formatting from one cell to another cell or range of cells. To do this, select the cell that contains the formatting you want to copy. Then click on the ⬚ tool. The mouse pointer changes to a special type of pointer:

Format Painting cursor

Move this pointer to select the cells into which you want the format copied. Click once on the left mouse button, and the format of the original cell is copied to the new cells. The mouse pointer returns to normal, and the display is updated.

Perhaps an example of using the Format Painter is in order. Let's assume that you have been working on a sheet for some time, and it looks like the one shown in Figure 19.1.

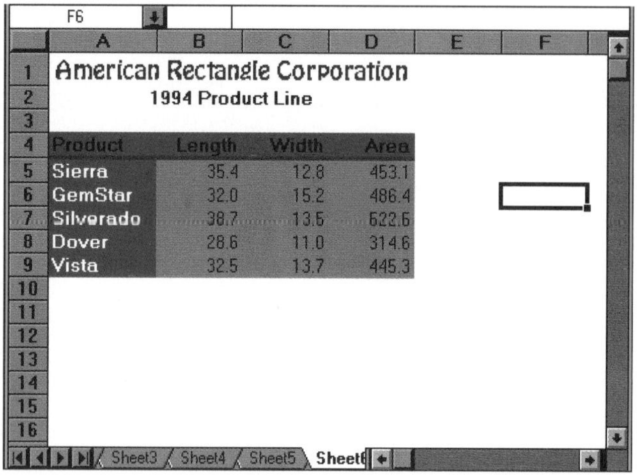

Figure 19.1 Your beginning sheet.

Now you are told that you need to add additional information in column E. Your boss wants you to include the perimeter of your 1994 rectangle offerings. So, you quickly add the title and put in the proper formulas to create the perimeters. Your sheet now looks like the one shown in Figure 19.2.

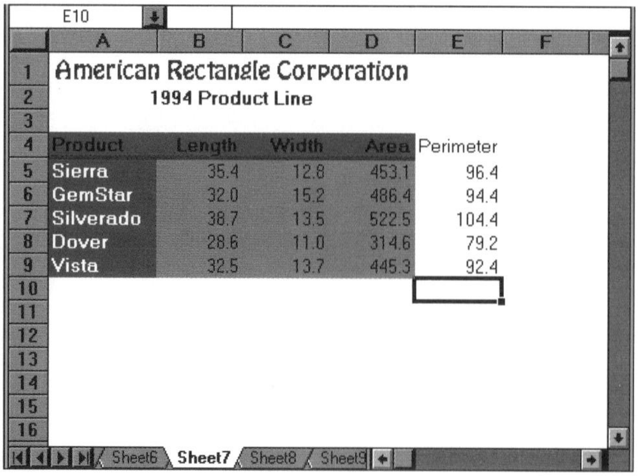

Figure 19.2 Your sheet after defining the Perimeter column.

The final step is to copy the formatting using the Format Painter. Select the cells at D4:D9, and click on the 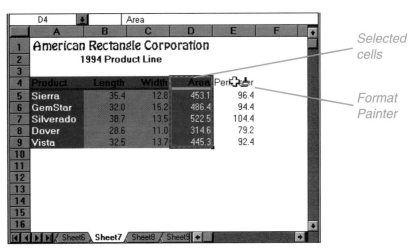 tool. Position the pointer used by the Format Painter over the cell at E4. Your sheet will appear as shown in Figure 19.3.

Figure 19.3 Ready to copy the formatting.

Click on the left mouse button, and the formatting is copied. In one simple step, your sheet is finished, appearing as shown in Figure 19.4. The only thing left to do is to adjust the column width on column E.

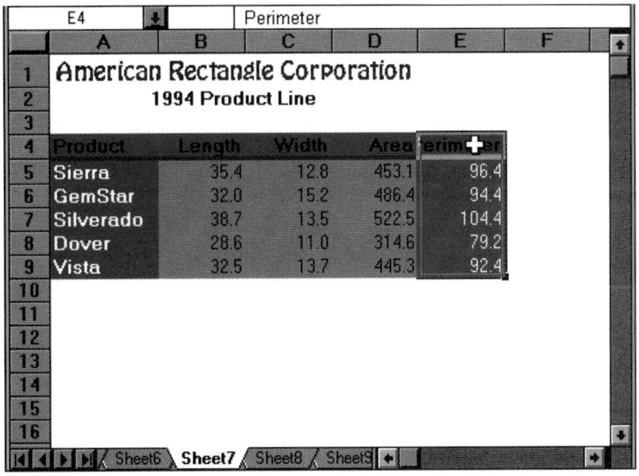

Figure 19.4 After using the Format Painter.

COPYING FROM ONE CELL TO MANY OTHER CELLS

You might wish to copy a format to more than one place in your workbook. Rather than choosing the ⬛ tool between each copy, simply double-click on the ⬛ tool. Again, the mouse pointer changes to indicate that the Format Painter is active. Select the cell or cells into which you want the format copied. Notice, however, that the Format Painter stays active even after you copy the format. You can continue to select cells as many times as necessary, and the format will be copied each time.

To turn off the Format Painter, click on the ⬛ tool again. The mouse pointer returns to normal.

PASTING FORMATS

There may be times when you don't want to use the Format Painter. For instance, you may have the standard toolbar turned off, and it would be a hassle to turn it on just to copy a format. In such cases, you can use copying and pasting to copy formats to a different cell or range of cells.

To copy formatting using this method, select the cell or cells whose format you wish to copy. Press CTRL-C or choose Copy from the Edit menu. (Copying was first introduced in Lesson 8.) Notice that a dotted, moving border appears around your selection.

The next step is to select the cell or cell range into which you want the formats pasted. Then choose Paste Special from the Edit menu and you will see the Paste Special dialog box, as in Figure 19.5:

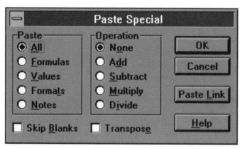

Figure 19.5 The Paste Special dialog box.

At the left side of the Paste Special dialog box, choose the Formats radio button and click on OK. The formatting from the original cells is copied into the new cells.

WHAT IS COPIED

When you copy formats, using either the Format Paintbrush or the pasting method, the following formats are copied:

- Character fonts
- Font size
- Text color
- Cell borders
- Cell color

- Cell pattern
- Number format
- Cell alignment
- Cell protection

Note: If there are multiple character formats contained within a cell, only the format of the first character is copied to the destination cells.

Notice, also, that only cell-related formats are copied. Excel does not copy other formats such as row height or column width.

WHAT YOU NEED TO KNOW

Once you learn how to copy formats, you can speed up formatting of your entire workbook quite a bit. In this lesson you have learned two general methods you can use to copy formats from one cell to another. You have learned:

- ☑ The Format Painter can be used to copy formats. First, select the cell that contains the formatting you want to copy. Then click on the ▨ tool and select the cell or cell range where you want the formatting copied.

- ☑ To use the Format Painter to format more than one cell or cell range, double-click on the ▨ tool. When you are through with copying formats, click on ▨ again to turn off the Format Painter.

- ☑ If you do not want to use the Format Painter, you can use the Paste Special option from the Edit menu to copy only formatting attributes between cells.

- ☑ When you copy formatting, not every formatting attribute is copied. In general, only those attributes which affect the particular cell or the information within the cell are copied.

In the next lesson you will learn how to use AutoFormat.

Lesson 20

Using AutoFormat

The past several lessons have taught you quite a bit about formatting your sheets and workbooks. You have learned how to work with cells, rows, columns, and the entire sheet in order to get the effect you want in your printed output. In this lesson you will learn how you can use the AutoFormat feature of Excel to simplify many of your routine formatting tasks. This lesson has been saved for last (as far as formatting is concerned) because it was important for you to learn the basics of formatting—how to do it manually—before you use the automatic formatting feature of Excel. In this lesson you will learn the following:

- What AutoFormat does

- How to use the AutoFormat feature

- Removing the effects of AutoFormat

- How to limit what AutoFormat does

WHAT AUTOFORMAT DOES

AutoFormat is a feature of Excel that allows you to format quickly an entire sheet or a portion thereof. This feature enables you to affect the overall layout of your table at one time. For instance, the table shown in Figure 20.1 was formatted with AutoFormat.

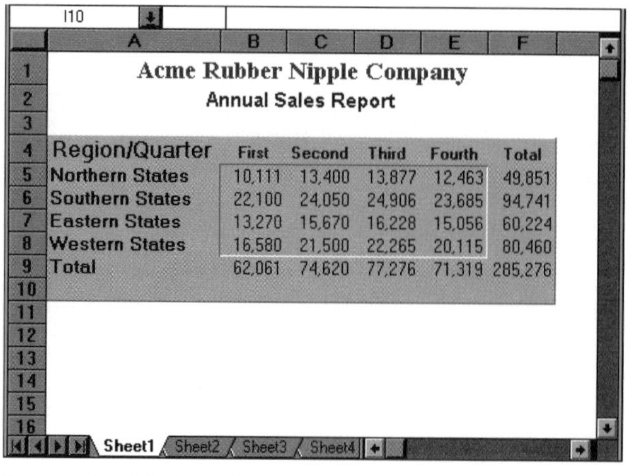

Figure 20.1 A table formatted with AutoFormat.

This entire format (except for the headings in rows 1 and 2) was done with one command. Excel formatted the cells, the numbers, and the column widths to produce this result.

HOW TO USE AUTOFORMAT

To use the AutoFormat command, all you need to do is make sure you select one of the following:

- A cell within the table you want to format

- A cell adjacent to the table you want to format

- The entire table you want to format

After you do this, choose the AutoFormat option from the Format menu. If you don't make one of the selections just listed, Excel will display an error message, shown in Figure 20.2.

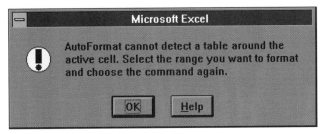

Figure 20.2 *An AutoFormat error message dialog box.*

If AutoFormat can find a table on which to work, you will see the AutoFormat dialog box, shown in Figure 20.3.

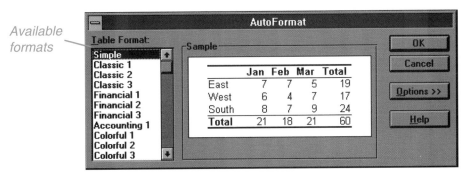

Figure 20.3 *The AutoFormat dialog box.*

In the Table Format list, there are 17 different formats that AutoFormat can apply. To get an idea of what each looks like, scroll through the list. The display in the Sample box will be updated every time you select a new format. When you find one that you like, click on OK and AutoFormat will make your table look like the sample. For example, the table displayed earlier in Figure 20.1 was formatted with the 3D Effects 1 format.

Quick Review

Excel's AutoFormat feature can save you time and energy when you need to format a table in your sheet. This feature applies color, number format, column width, font, and other attributes to make your table look like one of the available patterns. To use AutoFormat, follow these steps:

1. Select a cell in or around the table you want to format.

2. Choose the AutoFormat option from the Format menu.

3. Choose one of the predefined formats.

4. Press Enter or click on OK.

REMOVING THE EFFECTS OF AUTOFORMAT

After you apply an AutoFormat effect, you might decide that you don't like it. To make a change, all you need to do is choose AutoFormat again pick a different format. You can also choose Undo from the Edit menu or click on the Undo button (⟲) on the standard toolbar.

If you decide that you want to remove the formatting completely, choose AutoFormat and select the very last option in the Table Format list. This option, None, results in Excel removing all the formatting for the table.

You can also remove formatting by selecting the table and choosing Clear from the Edit menu. When you do, you will see a submenu appear:

Choose the Formats option, and Excel will remove all formatting from the cells.

No matter which method you use (AutoFormat or Clear), remember that only cell-related formatting is removed. Excel will not restore or change the column width or row height—even though they may have been changed by the AutoFormat command in the first place.

LIMITING WHAT AUTOFORMAT DOES

As you have already learned, AutoFormat affects just about every aspect of formatting a table. You might wish to limit the effects of the command, however. For instance, you might like how an AutoFormat table looks, but you don't want the number format changed. Or, you may have already spent a great deal of time adjusting the fonts used in each cell. If you accepted AutoFormat completely, all your work would be lost when the format was completed.

To limit what AutoFormat does, click on the `Options >>` button, available on the AutoFormat dialog box. When you do, the dialog box is enlarged, as shown in Figure 20.4:

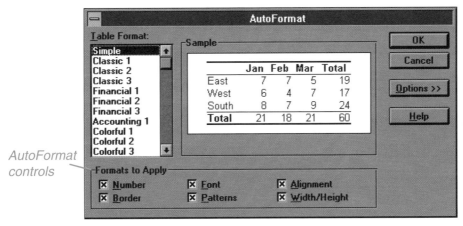

AutoFormat controls

Figure 20.4 *The AutoFormat dialog box showing format options.*

There are six options displayed in this enlarged dialog box. Each option controls a different formatting area that AutoFormat can change. If you don't want that particular area affected, click on the check box beside the option to disable it. Turning a check box on or off also affects the formatting sample shown in the dialog box.

As an example, suppose you didn't want the fonts affected by AutoFormat. In this case, you would disable the Font option. Later, when you click on [OK], AutoFormat will change all those areas except the ones you have specifically disallowed.

WHAT YOU NEED TO KNOW

AutoFormat is a powerful formatting tool provided with Excel. By using AutoFormat, you can change every aspect of a table's format, all with the click of a single button. In this lesson you have learned how you can use AutoFormat to enhance your workbooks. You have learned:

☑ AutoFormat is a tool that assists you in formatting an entire table at one time.

☑ Using AutoFormat is as easy as selecting a portion of the data table and then choosing the AutoFormat option from the Format menu. Select a table format and click on [OK]

☑ Excel provides several different methods you can use to remove formatting from a cell or group of cells.

☑ If you don't want AutoFormat to affect everything within your data table, you can control what is changed by clicking on the [Options >>] button when the AutoFormat dialog box is displayed.

This concludes the formatting lessons. You now know everything you need to make your workbooks look their best. In the next lesson you will begin to learn how to control the Excel environment.

Section Four

CONTROLLING YOUR ENVIRONMENT

Excel gives you a great deal of flexibility in controlling what you see and how Excel works. In this section you will learn how you can control what the display looks like, how Excel calculates your workbook, how you can protect your work, and how you can save and quickly recall views of your information. By applying the procedures and techniques described in this section, you will begin to learn how to tailor Excel to work closer to the way you want to work

Lesson 21

Controlling the Display

So far you have learned how to present information effectively with Excel. This lesson starts a new section and changes the focus a bit. Here you will learn how you can begin to control the Excel environment. In particular, this lesson focuses on how you can change the way Excel displays your information. You will learn how to

- Control gridlines

- Hide row and column headers

- Turn off display of zero values

- Display formulas

- Display page breaks

- Rename sheets in your workbook

- Turn off the sheet tabs

WHAT SHOULD BE DISPLAYED?

Excel provides quite a bit of latitude in controlling what shows up on your screen. You can direct Excel either to include or exclude many helpful items, depending on your needs. To control what is displayed, you need to choose Options from the Tools menu. When you do, you will see the Options dialog box, as in Figure 21.1; make sure the View file card is selected.

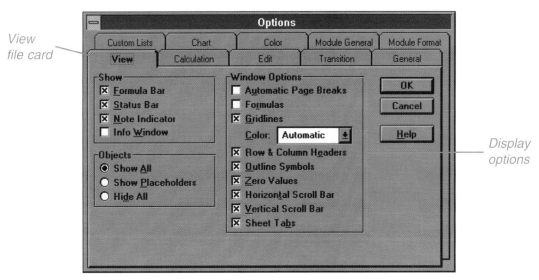

View
file card

Display
options

Figure 21.1 *The Options dialog box, showing the View file card.*

The following sections describe the important items you can control from this dialog box.

DISPLAY GRIDLINES

You know what gridlines are; they have been shown in many of the illustrations in this book. An example is shown in Figure 21.2.

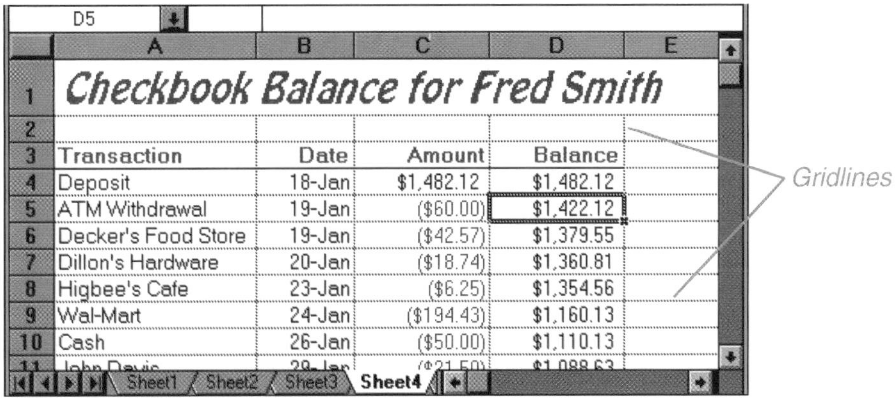

Gridlines

Figure 21.2 *A sheet with gridlines turned on.*

You might not have noticed, but many other illustrations did not include gridlines. You can turn gridlines on and off by using the Gridlines check box:

x enables gridlines ⎯⎯⎯

☒ Gridlines

Whether you uses gridlines or not is up to you. Personally, I prefer to view my data without gridlines; I find them distracting. While it is possible to change the color of the gridlines so they are not so noticeable, they are still there and distract my eye from what my final sheet will appear like when it is printed.

That brings up an important point to remember—changing this gridline setting does not change whether gridlines are printed or not. That is done using the Page Setup command, as described in Lesson 17. If you want what is displayed to most accurately match what will print, you will want to make sure that the display of gridlines is set the same as the printing of gridlines.

Row and Column Headers

Row and column headers are quite useful in Excel. They are the quickest way to select a row or column, and they always give you an idea of the location of your data. Figure 21.3 shows an example of row and column headers, although you could also find them in practically every other illustration in this book.

Column headers

Row headers

	A	B	C	D	E	F
	L13					
2						
3	State	1991	1992	1993	3-Yr Growth	
4	Arkansas	9,743	15,162	25,226	158.91%	
5	Colorado	13,836	21,458	27,345	97.64%	
6	Florida	15,939	28,137	36,831	131.07%	
7	Georgia	48,540	50,915	56,741	16.90%	
8	Indiana	14,022	18,820	32,437	131.33%	
9	Kentucky	12,579	19,556	34,568	174.81%	
10	New York	21,817	37,672	41,901	92.06%	
11	Ohio	24,156	40,107	62,439	158.48%	
12	Oregon	17,968	22,291	34,568	92.39%	
13	Pennsylvania	23,021	24,917	43,813	90.32%	
14	Texas	36,049	43,325	51,574	43.07%	
15	Wyoming	12,336	16,210	23,143	87.61%	
16	Totals	250,006	338,570	470,586	88.23%	
17						

Sheet2 / Sheet3 / Sheet4 \ **Sheet5** / Sh

Figure 21.3 The location of row and column headers.

You cannot turn row and column headers off individually; they are both either on or off. You control them by using the Row & Column Headers check box:

x enables Row & Column Headers

If you turn off row and column headers, you have more room to display data from your sheet, but many users find that a small compensation for not being able to see easily the cell in which data is located. Typically, turning off row and column headers is of the most value when you are using Excel to create slide shows and other presentation material that will use the screen. (Unfortunately, creating slide shows with Excel is beyond the scope of this book. When you are comfortable with the day-to-day basics of using the program, you might want to experiment with this capability.)

CELLS WITH ZERO VALUES

You might not use this option often, but there are circumstances where it is very helpful. When you start with a new Excel workbook, every cell is blank—all of them are empty. As you add values, text, and formulas, things start appearing in your workbook. (That's the idea, isn't it?) If you enter a formula, and the result of that formula is 0, or if you enter a 0 into a cell, Excel displays that value. However, if you are using a sheet that has a great number of 0s, they can be distracting from the meaningful data in the sheet. Figure 21.4 shows an example of such a case.

Account Name	Jan-93	Feb-93	Mar-93	Apr-93	May-93	Jun-93	Jul-93
					Galbraith & So		
					Recap of Accounts		
AAA Carpet	235.20	0.00	0.00	834.90	0.00	0.00	0.00
Aaron Tents	0.00	921.30	0.00	0.00	1,765.00	0.00	0.00
Bingo Lanes	0.00	0.00	545.55	0.00	0.00	0.00	0.00
Brown Shoes	0.00	0.00	435.93	0.00	0.00	0.00	0.00
Chez Gault Catering	134.60	0.00	0.00	0.00	0.00	0.00	0.00
Deeter's Pub	600.00	0.00	0.00	0.00	0.00	0.00	600.00
Garrison Welding	543.10	289.20	912.60	104.20	692.15	345.70	462.80
Givens Electric	2,345.60	3,918.32	2,954.82	4,597.65	4,271.00	5,256.40	5,439.10
Hawkeye Greenhouse	7,833.00	0.00	0.00	0.00	0.00	0.00	0.00
Jingle Jones	0.00	0.00	0.00	0.00	0.00	0.00	0.00
KQWX Radio	325.00	0.00	0.00	325.00	0.00	0.00	325.00
Pipes 'n Pizza	0.00	82.10	0.00	0.00	0.00	102.45	0.00

Sheet5 / Sheet6 / Sheet7 / Sheet8 / Sheet9 / Sheet1

Figure 21.4 An example of 0s concealing the real data.

To overcome this problem, you can turn the 0s off. This is done by using the Zero Values check box:

When you turn off the zero values, then Excel "blanks out" every cell that contains either 0 or a zero result. This means your data is much more readable, but it also means it is harder to spot cells that actually contain a formula or a value. Figure 21.5 shows what the sheet in Figure 21.4 looks like if Zero Values is turned off.

	A	B	C	D	E	F	G	H
						Galbraith & So		
1								
2						Recap of Accounts		
3								
4	Account Name	Jan-93	Feb-93	Mar-93	Apr-93	May-93	Jun-93	Jul-93
5	AAA Carpet	235.20			834.90			
6	Aaron Tents		921.30			1,765.00		
7	Bingo Lanes			545.55				
8	Brown Shoes			435.93				
9	Chez Gault Catering	134.60						
10	Deeter's Pub	600.00						600.00
11	Garrison Welding	543.10	289.20	912.60	104.20	692.15	345.70	462.80
12	Givens Electric	2,345.60	3,918.32	2,954.82	4,597.65	4,271.00	5,256.40	5,439.10
13	Hawkeye Greenhouse	7,833.00						
14	Jingle Jones							
15	KQWX Radio	325.00			325.00			325.00
16	Pipes 'n Pizza		82.10				102.45	

Figure 21.5 With Zero Values turned off, some data is much more readable.

FORMULAS VERSUS RESULTS

You learned about formulas way back in Lesson 7. By default, Excel shows the result of all formulas you enter in your workbook. There may be times, however, when you don't want to see the results of a formula, but you want to see the formula itself. This is done by using the Formulas check box:

If you select this option, the results of your formulas are not shown. Instead, the formulas themselves are displayed, as shown in Figure 21.6.

	A	B	C	D
2		1994 Product Line		
3				
4	Product	Length	Width	Area
5	Sierra	35.4	12.8	=B5:B9*C5:C9
6	GemStar	32	15.2	=B5:B9*C5:C9
7	Silverado	38.7	13.5	=B5:B9*C5:C9
8	Dover	28.6	11	=B5:B9*C5:C9
9	Vista	32.5	13.7	=B5:B9*C5:C9
10				
11				
12				

Sheet2 / Sheet3 / Sheet4 / Sheet5 \ **Sheet6** / S

Figure 21.6 An example sheet with formulas displayed.

AUTOMATIC PAGE BREAKS

As you format your sheets, Excel keeps track of where page breaks should occur, based on the page setup settings you have used (see Lesson 13 and Lesson 17). Normally, these page breaks are not displayed by Excel. Instead, you need to use Page Preview mode (Lesson 13) to determine where a page will break. You can, however, instruct Excel to show you where page breaks will occur. This is controlled by the Automatic Page Breaks check box:

× *displays auto-matic page breaks*

When you select this, page breaks will appear as dashed lines on your sheet. These dashed lines do not print, they only show up on the display.

The value of using this option will depend, many times, on how you have your sheets formatted. If you use lots of dark lines or patterns, they might obscure the page breaks. In such instances, you will need to examine your sheets more closely than normal to determine where page breaks are located.

SHEET TABS

In Lesson 4 you learned about the Excel environment. One of the standard items you were introduced to was sheet tabs. These appear across the bottom of your screen, and represent individual sheets available within your workbook:

Excel allows you to change the names assigned to sheet tabs and to control their display. The next two sections describe how to do this.

CHANGING THE NAME OF SHEET TABS

When you first open a workbook, the sheets in the new workbook use generic names such as Sheet1, Sheet2, Sheet3, and so on. Excel allows you to change these names in one of two ways. The easiest way is to use the mouse to double-click on the sheet tab. When you do, you will see the Rename Sheet dialog box, as shown in Figure 21.7:

Figure 21.7 The Rename Sheet dialog box.

Change the name, and when you press ENTER or click on [OK], Excel updates the sheet tabs to reflect the new name:

Changed sheet name

The other way to change the name of a sheet is to select the sheet whose name you want to change, and then choose Sheet from the Format menu. You will then see a submenu:

Select the Rename option, and you will see the same Rename Sheet dialog box you just saw.

DISPLAYING SHEET TABS

Some people like having the sheet tabs displayed. They are particularly helpful if you are using multiple sheets in your workbook. They make switching between sheets very quick and easy. If you find yourself working with only one sheet, or you would rather display more data than take up space displaying sheet tabs, you can turn them off. This is done by selecting Options from the Tools menu, making sure the View file card is displayed, as in Figure 21.8.

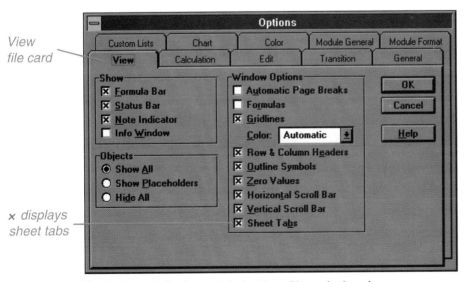

Figure 21.8 The Options dialog box, with the View file card selected.

The Sheet Tabs check box controls whether the sheet tabs are displayed or not. Make your selection and click on [OK]

WHAT YOU NEED TO KNOW

Excel allows you a great deal of control over how your screen appears. In this lesson you have learned how you can control your display. In particular, you have learned the following:

☑ To control the display characteristics used by Excel, you can choose Options from the Tools menu. There are many characteristics you can choose from the resultant dialog box.

☑ Gridlines are helpful when entering numbers in a sheet, but may be distracting with some types of information. Excel allows you to turn gridlines on or off.

☑ You can turn off row and column headers, which is particularly helpful if you are using Excel to do an on-screen presentation.

☑ Zero values, while helpful in some situations, can be distracting if there are too many of them in your sheet. You can instruct Excel to turn off the display of zero values.

☑ Normally, Excel displays the results of any formulas contained in your sheet. You can, however, instruct Excel to display formulas instead of their results.

☑ Excel allows you to easily turn other display characteristics on or off, such as automatic page breaks and sheet tabs.

☑ You can quickly rename the label appearing on the sheet tabs by double-clicking on the sheet tab you want to rename.

In the next lesson you will learn how to control the way Excel calculates formulas, automatically or manually, and to what degree of precision.

Lesson 22

Controlling How Excel Calculates

Many of the sheets and workbooks you create will, by their very nature, be simple. Others will be large and complex, or may become that way over time. As you develop more complex sheets, you might find that Excel slows down a bit. This is usually because there are many, many formulas that need to be calculated every time you change a value. To overcome this, Excel allows you to completely control when and how calculation is performed. This lesson deals with how you calculate your sheets. You will learn how to

- Control automatic calculation
- Calculate your sheets and workbook manually
- Turn off calculation before saving
- Control the precision of calculation

AUTOMATIC CALCULATION

By default, Excel calculates your entire workbook every time you change a value, formula, or text within any sheet of that workbook. It also performs a recalculation if you change a name. Actually, not every cell is recalculated—that would take too long. Excel attempts to update only those cells that are related to the changed value, formula, text, or name.

As your workbooks become larger and more complex, you may find that even this amount of calculation slows Excel down to the point where it is either distracting or hard to accomplish your work. For this reason, you can turn automatic calculation on or off. This is done by choosing Options from the Tools menu, making sure the Calculation file card is displayed. The Options dialog box will appear, as in Figure 22.1.

Notice in the upper-left corner of the dialog box, the Automatic option is selected. This is the default condition of Excel. You can change to one of the other choices available, if desired. For instance, you could choose Automatic Except Tables if you find you have many, many data tables in your workbook. In this circumstance, you would find that you could enter data quicker with this option selected.

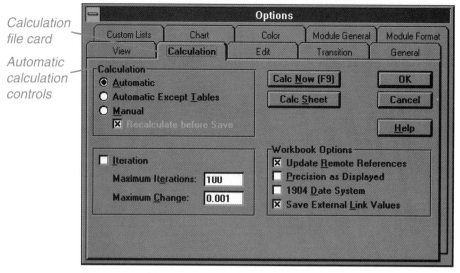

Calculation file card

Automatic calculation controls

Figure 22.1 *The Options dialog box, with Calculation file card displayed.*

The final option in this section, Manual, can be selected if you don't want Excel to perform any calculations on its own. In this case, you must recalculate manually, as described in the next section.

CALCULATING YOUR WORKBOOK MANUALLY

If you limit automatic calculation in any way, you will need to remember to manually calculate your workbook whenever you want to see the effects of any data changes you have made. There are two ways you can do this. The first is to press **F9** or **CTRL-=**. The second involves choosing Options from the Tools menu, making sure the Calculation file card is displayed. If you click on the Calc Now (F9) button, every open workbook is updated.

Remember that, depending on the complexity of your workbook, calculation might take some time to perform. Be patient, and recalculate only when you need to. If you find yourself recalculating often, it might be better to turn automatic calculation back on.

MANUALLY CALCULATING A SINGLE SHEET

If your workbook contains many different sheets, each complex in its own right, your calculation burdens are the greatest for Excel to bear. In these instances, you might want to calculate only the current sheet, instead of an entire workbook. As with the method of manual calculation described in the previous section, there are two ways to accomplish this. The first is to press SHIFT-F9. The second is to choose Options from the Tools menu, and then select the Calculation file card. If you click on the ▨ Calc Sheet button, your current sheet is updated.

Remember that only the current sheet is calculated and updated. If you later switch to another sheet, you might want to calculate it manually before assuming that anything it contains is correct.

QUICK REVIEW

If you turn off automatic calculation in Excel, there are several ways you can manually instruct Excel to calculate your workbook. You can choose either of the following, based on how extensive you want the calculation to be:

- Press **F9** or CTRL-= to calculate the entire workbook.

- Press SHIFT-**F9** to calculate only the current sheet.

CALCULATING BEFORE SAVING

It is possible within Excel to *link* workbooks. This means that the formulas in one workbook will be dependent on the values or results in another workbook. When you save a workbook, Excel calculates the sheets in that workbook one last time so that the file always represents the most up-to-date results. This ensures that any other workbooks that reference the saved file will always have the most up-to-date information available.

If you have automatic calculation enabled, this whole area will be of little concern, because Excel takes care of it all automatically. However, if you have selected manual calculation, this becomes a bigger issue. Notice, in the Options dialog box with the Calculation file card, that under the Manual calculation option, there is a choice as to whether the workbook is recalculated before it is saved:

× recalculates before saving

You should understand that if you turn off this option (recalculating before saving), your file saves will happen faster. However, the information saved to disk will not be updated, and other workbooks, which might depend on that information, might not be correct because the information in this workbook is not up to date. To many users, this might not be a big deal. If you use quite a few linked workbooks, however, it can affect the overall accuracy of your workbook data.

CALCULATION PRECISION

There is one other topic about calculation that is of interest. You already know that Excel maintains information internally to a precision of 15 decimal places. Remember that this is independent of the precision used to display a value. This very accurate precision is used in the calculations that Excel performs. As you might expect, this level of precision takes time, particularly if there are many, many formulas in your sheet.

You can instruct Excel to limit the precision it uses in performing calculations. This is done by choosing Options from the Tools menu, making sure the Calculation file card is displayed. In the bottom-right section of the dialog box is the control for calculation precision:

✕ uses precision
as displayed

If you choose this option, Excel will only use the precision displayed in your sheet to perform calculations. For instance, if a value is stored as 19.23675, but is displayed as 19.24, then the latter value is used in the calculation. This is faster, but it can lead to some errors in calculations that could be compounded over the course of calculating an entire sheet.

Remember, however, that Excel still maintains the very accurate 15-decimal place precision internally; only the calculations are affected. If you later turn off this option, the more accurate calculations will be resumed.

WHAT YOU NEED TO KNOW

Performing calculations is Excel's forte. However, there are circumstances in which you might want to modify how and when Excel does its calculations. In this lesson you have learned how you can control this important behind-the-scenes aspect of Excel. You have learned the following:

☑ If you have large spreadsheets that take a long time to calculate, you may want to turn automatic calculation off.

☑ If you have turned off automatic calculation, you can manually calculate a workbook by pressing **F9** or **CTRL-=**.

☑ If you don't want to manually calculate your entire workbook, you can calculate a single sheet by pressing **SHIFT-F9**.

☑ If you use workbooks that are linked to each other, it is important to recalculate before saving. If you do not, then it is possible that information in related workbooks will not be correct.

☑ Normally Excel performs all operations to 15 digits of precision. You can, however, instruct Excel to use only the precision displayed on the sheet. Doing so will speed up the calculation process.

In the next lesson you will learn how to protect your work—including your whole workbook, sheets, or individual cells.

Lesson 23

Protecting Your Work

It is not uncommon that workbooks developed by one person will be used by many other people. As anyone who uses Excel is aware, defining the relationships between cells, as described in formulas, is the most time-consuming task you perform when building a workbook. When other people use your workbook, it is possible for them to ruin much of your work by accidentally changing a formula here or there.

To protect against this possibility, Excel allows you to protect your work. In this lesson you will learn how that is done. You will learn how to

- Protect an Excel file
- Hide sheets
- Protect individual cells
- Protect a sheet
- Protect a workbook

PROTECTING AN UNOPENED WORKBOOK

The most secure level of protection you can employ is to protect the entire Excel file. There are several types of protection available at this level. You can do any of the following:

- Require a password to open the file
- Require a password to save the file
- Suggest strongly that a file be opened as read-only

Each of these options is specified when a workbook is first saved. How this is done and the effects are described in the following sections.

REQUIRING A PASSWORD WHEN OPENING

When you first save a workbook, you will see the Save As dialog box (described in Lesson 11), shown in Figure 23.1

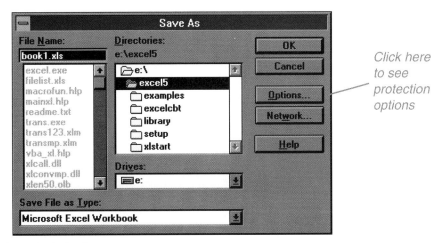

Figure 23.1 *The Save As dialog box.*

If you click on the Options... button, you will see the Save Options dialog box, shown in Figure 23.2.

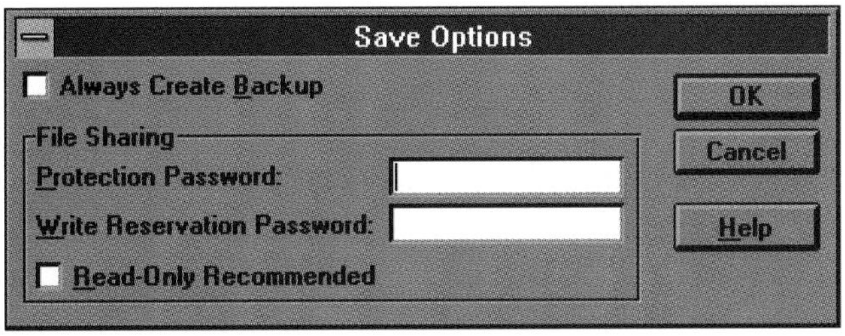

Figure 23.2 *The Save Options dialog box.*

To protect the workbook so that only authorized people can load it, enter a password in the Protection Password field. When you press ENTER or click on OK, you are asked to confirm your password, as shown in Figure 23.3.

Figure 23.3 *The Confirm Password dialog box.*

167

Make sure you enter your password the same was as you did the first time. When you press ENTER or click on ███OK███, the file is saved, using the password you specified.

Note: *You should make sure that you remember your password or write it down in a secure place. If you forget the password, you will never be able to access the data in this workbook again.*

When you attempt later to reload this workbook, you are asked to enter the password, as shown in Figure 23.4.

Figure 23.4 The Password dialog box.

Enter the correct password, and the file is loaded. If you enter the wrong one, you are informed, and the workbook is not loaded.

REQUIRING A PASSWORD WHEN SAVING

Excel also allows you to set a password that is required when saving a workbook. This is a great improvement over previous versions of Excel. It results in keeping the original version of your workbook safe, unless the user knows the password. If they do not know the password, they must save the modified workbook under a new name.

To institute this type of password, you start to follow the same steps described in the previous section. When you see the Save Options dialog box, enter a password in the Write Reservation Password field. When you press ENTER or click on ███OK███, you will be asked to confirm the password.

Now, anyone can still load the workbook. They will, however, see the dialog box shown in Figure 23.5 when they load. If you have the password, you can enter it and use the file as normal. If you do not, the file must be loaded as read-only.

Figure 23.5 *Asking for a password when you load a workbook.*

SUGGESTING THAT A FILE BE READ-ONLY

One level down from the protection method described in the previous section is suggesting that a file be opened as read-only. Some users might not even classify this as protection, since it does not prevent the user from loading and changing a workbook. It does, however, let the user know that it is important to not change the workbook. From there on, it is up to the good sense of the user to not make any changes to the original file.

To use this type of protection, you start to follow the same steps described in the previous sections. When you see the Save Options dialog box, select the Read-Only Recommended check box. Then, press ENTER or click on OK to save the file.

When someone tries to open the workbook, they will see a dialog box, shown in Figure 23.6, recommending that the file be opened as read-only.

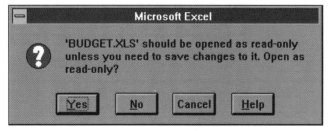

Figure 23.6 *Excel's recommendation to load a file as read-only.*

If the user clicks on Yes, the file is opened as read-only; if they click on No, it is opened as normal, and the user can overwrite the original file.

PROTECTING AN OPEN WORKBOOK

Once a workbook is open, there are additional steps you can take to protect your work. You can protect the entire workbook, individual sheets, and even cells on those sheets. These procedures are described in the following sections.

HIDING SHEETS

Before delving into the world of locking, unlocking, and applying passwords, it would be good to remember that not all protection requires passwords. You can also hide sheets so they are not readily accessible. These sheets can contain information and formulas which are accessed from the visible sheets, but it is harder for people to get to them and change them.

To hide a sheet, you first select the sheet you want to hide. Then select the Sheet option from the Format menu. You will see a submenu:

Choose Hide, and the current sheet disappears. It is not gone forever; it is simply hidden from view. If you later want to unhide the sheet, choose the Unhide option from the Sheet submenu from the Format menu. You will see the Unhide dialog box, shown in Figure 23.7.

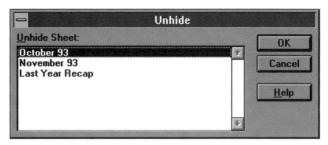

Figure 23.7 The Unhide dialog box.

Select the sheet you again want to display, and then press ENTER or click on ▭OK▭. The sheet is again displayed, in its original position in relation to other sheets in the workbook.

PROTECTING CELLS

The first line of defense in protecting formulas or other valuable information is to make sure that the cells containing that information are locked. While individual cells in a sheet cannot be password-protected, this locking and unlocking process works in conjunction with the password you apply to an entire sheet. (This is described more fully in the following section.)

By default, all cells within a sheet are locked. To unlock a range of cells, which means they can be changed even if the sheet is protected, you should first select the range you want to unlock. Once this is done, choose Cell from the Format menu, making sure the Protection file card is displayed. The Format Cells dialog box appears, as in Figure 23.8.

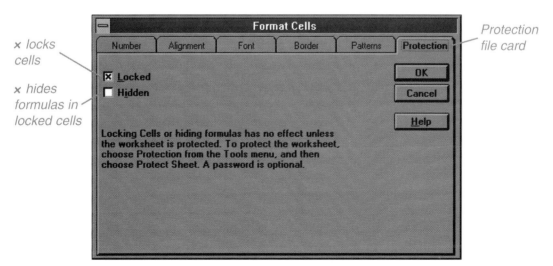

Figure 23.8 The Format Cells dialog box.

Make sure that the Locked check box reflects the condition you want for the selected cells. You can also (if the cells are locked) choose the Hidden check box. This effectively turns off a part of the formula bar for locked cells. Normally, when a cell is selected, Excel displays the contents of that cell on the formula bar. When this option is selected, and the user later selects a locked cell on a protected sheet, the formula is not displayed on the formula bar.

PROTECTING SHEETS

Protecting an entire sheet works hand in hand with protecting cells, as described in the previous section. Once you have defined which cells are to be locked (remember; all cells are originally locked unless you explicitly unlock them), you should select the Protection option from the Tools menu. You will then see a submenu:

Choose the Protect Sheet option, and you will see the Protect Sheet dialog box, as shown in Figure 23.9.

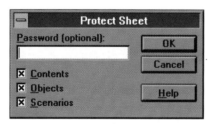

Figure 23.9 *The Protect Sheet dialog box.*

In the Password field, you should supply a password that you want used to protect this sheet. There are also three choices in the dialog box, which control what, exactly, is protected.

- **Contents** The contents of each locked cell are protected from being changed.

- **Objects** Each locked graphical object on the sheet is protected from being changed.

- **Scenarios** Each scenario developed on the sheet is protected from being changed. (Scenarios are beyond the scope of this book.)

When you press ENTER or click on , you are asked to reconfirm your password. Once this is done, the sheet is protected. Remember that if your workbook contains multiple sheets, you might want to protect each of them. You can either use the same password or different passwords for each sheet in your workbook.

If you later want to unprotect a sheet, you must again choose the Protection option from the Tools menu. This time, however, the submenu has changed:

Choose Unprotect Sheet, and you will see the Unprotect Sheet dialog box, as shown in Figure 23.10.

Figure 23.10 The Unprotect Sheet dialog box.

To unprotect the sheet, enter the password you entered previously to protect the sheet. When you enter the correct password and press ENTER or click on , you will again have full access to all parts of the sheet.

PROTECTING WORKBOOKS

Protecting a workbook is not quite as involved as protecting a sheet. To protect a workbook, you choose the Protection option from the Tools menu. When you do, you will see a submenu:

Choose the Protect Workbook option, and you will see the Protect Workbook dialog box, shown in Figure 23.11

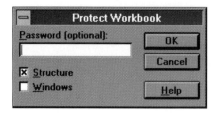

Figure 23.11 *The Protect Workbook dialog box.*

In the Password field, you should supply a password that you want used to protect this workbook. Notice that there are two options provided in the dialog box that are used to indicate what to protect. Excel allows you to protect the workbook Structure, which means that a user cannot change the name, order, or number of sheets in the workbook. You can also protect workbook Windows, which means the sizing, positioning, status (hidden or unhidden) of each sheet in the workbook.

When you press ENTER or click on , you are asked to reconfirm your password. Once this is done, the workbook is protected. If you want later to unprotect the workbook, you must again choose the Protection option from the Tools menu. The submenu will reflect the current condition of the workbook:

Choose Unprotect Workbook, and you will see the Unprotect Workbook dialog box, as shown in Figure 23.12.

Figure 23.12 *The Unprotect Workbook dialog box.*

To unprotect the workbook, enter the password you previously entered to protect it. When you enter the correct password and press ENTER or click on OK, you will again have full access to all parts of the workbook.

QUICK REVIEW

Once a sheet is open, your work can still be protected. For instance, you can hide entire sheets within the workbook, or you can protect cells, sheets, or workbooks. To hide a sheet, you select Sheet from the Format menu, and then choose Hide.

Protecting cells is done in conjunction with protecting sheets. You protect cells by first selecting the cells you want to protect, and then choosing Cell from the Format menu. On the Protection file card you can choose to lock or unlock the cells. When you later protect the sheet (by choosing Protection from the Tools menu, and then selecting Protect Sheet), the locked cells cannot be changed.

Finally, protecting a workbook means that Excel will not allow anyone to change the structure and possibly window organization of your workbook. This is done by choosing Protection from the Tools menu and then selecting Protect Workbook.

WHAT YOU NEED TO KNOW

For many people, protecting their sheets and workbooks is a very important matter. Excel provides you with many different methods of protecting your worksheet. You can protect anything from individual cells to the file itself. In this lesson you have learned the following:

- ☑ You can protect an unopened workbook by requiring a password either when opening or saving the file, or by instructing Excel to suggest that a file be opened as read-only.

- ☑ You can protect sheets within an open workbook by hiding sheets, locking cells within a sheet, and using a password to protect individual sheets.

- ☑ The sizing, position, and status of each sheet within a workbook can be protected by assigning a password to an entire workbook.

In the next lesson you will learn about using the View Manager to store and retrieve complex views of your workbook.

Lesson 24

Using the View Manager

One of the features provided with Excel is the View Manager. This add-in program provides you with the capability to store and retrieve complex views of your sheet easily. In this lesson you will learn how you can use the View Manager to make Excel even more productive. You will learn:

- What a view is

- How to ensure that the View Manager is loaded

- How to define and delete a view

- How to use a view

WHAT IS A VIEW?

In Excel, a *view* is a stored pattern of what the information in a sheet should look like. It contains information such as which rows and columns are visible, row height, column width, formatting characteristics, and window size and position. For instance, you could have several views of data in a sheet. One view could show the entire sheet, while another could show a condensed-view of the information. Still another could be used to show the full sheet on the screen at one time.

MAKING SURE THE VIEW MANAGER IS INSTALLED

The View Manager is not part of the base Excel system. Instead, it is an add-in that can be added to or removed from Excel, based on your needs. Typically, the View Manager is installed and enabled when you first install Excel. If you have had other users who use your system, they might have disabled the View Manager. The easiest way to see if the View Manager is available is to pull down the View menu:

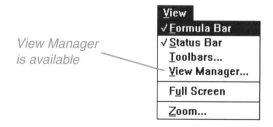

View Manager
is available

If there is a choice for View Manager on the menu, then this add-in has been enabled. If not, then you will need to select the Add-Ins option from the Tools menu. You will then see the Add-ins dialog box, as in Figure 24.1.

Enable this
option to use
View Manager

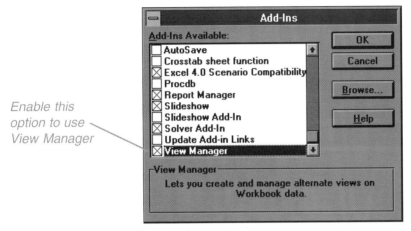

Figure 24.1 *The Add-ins dialog box.*

Select the View Manager option (make sure the check box is selected) and then click on ▮ OK ▮. The View Manager should now be available; you can check the View menu again to make sure.

ADDING VIEWS

To add a view to the View Manager, you must first format and situate your sheet as you want it to appear. Once this is done, select the View Manager option from the View menu. When you do, you will see the View Manager dialog box, as in Figure 24.2.

Figure 24.2 *The View Manager.*

To define a new view, click on the Add... button and you will see the Add View dialog box, shown in Figure 24.3.

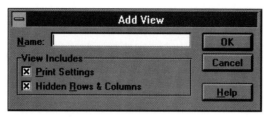

Figure 24.3 The Add View dialog box.

Supply the name you want associated with this view and make sure you select the options that reflect what you want saved with this view. Then click on OK, and the current view (what your sheet looks like) is saved by Excel.

You can now proceed to situation your sheet so it reflects what you want saved as the next view. Repeat this process to store the new view.

USING STORED VIEWS

Once you have defined the views for a sheet, you can use them to look quickly at your information in different ways. To select different views, choose the View Manager option from the View menu. When you do, you will see the View Manager dialog box, as shown in Figure 24.4.

List of defined views for the workbook

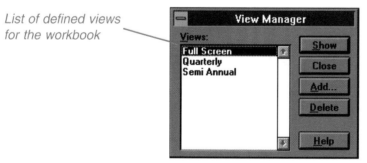

Figure 24.4 Choosing a view from the View Manager.

Select a view from those listed and click on [Show]. Your Excel display settings are changed to reflect what was previously saved in the view.

DELETING VIEWS

After you have finished with a project, or if the structure of your sheet changes enough, you might want to delete some previously defined views. To do this, select the View Manager option from the View menu. You will then see the View Manager dialog box. Select the view you want to delete and then click on the [Delete] button. The view is removed from the list of those available.

WHAT YOU NEED TO KNOW

Excel is a powerful spreadsheet program that lets you examine your data in many different ways. You may want to save some of those ways so that you can call them up at a later time. The View Manager is designed to allow you to do just that. In this lesson you have learned how to use the View Manager. You have learned the following:

☑ A view is a pattern of what information within a sheet should look like. This includes settings such as the rows and columns which are visible, row height, column width, formatting characteristics, and window sizing.

☑ The View Manager is an Excel add-on that must be installed before it can be used. If there is a View Manager option on the View menu, then it is installed.

☑ To add a view, you first format your sheet the way you want it to appear. Then choose View Manager from the View menu and click on the [Add...] button.

☑ To show a view you previously defined, choose View Manager from the View menu, select the named view, and click on the [Show] button.

☑ To delete a view you previously defined, choose View Manager from the View menu, select the named view, and click on the [Delete] button.

In the next lesson you will start to learn about the many shortcuts you can use in Excel.

Section Five

WORKING WITH CHARTS

So far you have learned how to work with sheets and workbooks strictly from a numbers-only perspective. Excel has a more colorful side, however, in which you can quickly and easily create charts to graphically present your data. These charts can range from simple line charts to complex three-dimensional surface graphs. Excel allows you to create them all with the touch of only a few buttons. Not only will you learn how to do this, but you will also learn how to go "one step beyond" and change the appearance of different parts of your chart. Finally, you will learn the differences between printing charts and printing regular workbooks.

Lesson 25

Creating a Chart

So far in this book you have learned to use the powerful spreadsheet features of Excel. Excel also contains an equally powerful chart capability, which is introduced in this lesson. Here you will learn

- What a chart is

- How to create an embedded chart

- How to create a chart sheet

WHAT IS A CHART?

In Excel, a *chart* is a graphical representation of the data contained within a sheet. This presupposes, of course, that your sheet contains numeric values that can be graphed. Each cell is converted into a *datapoint,* which is at the intersection of an X and Y axis for two-dimensional charts or an X, Y, and Z axis for three-dimensional charts. This datapoint can be expressed in any number of graphic styles, including bars, columns, lines, and pie wedges. (You will learn more about chart types in Lesson 26.)

There are two general ways you can create a chart in Excel. The first is to create an *embedded chart*—one that appears within a sheet of information. These are best used when creating reports and other documents that must have the graphic information included with other types of information, such as text explanations or raw figures.

The other way to create a chart is to create a *chart sheet*—one that appears on its own sheet within a workbook. These are best used when the graphic speaks for itself or when you are creating slides or overheads.

CREATING AN EMBEDDED CHART

The easiest way to create an embedded chart is to select the data you want in the chart, and then click on the ChartWizard tool ( ) on the standard toolbar. For instance, suppose you wanted to chart the information shown in the sheet in Figure 25.1. You would first select the data range to be charted—in this case A3:D15. Notice that no summary or total information is included in this range. You will create the best charts when you work with raw data; in this case, the sales figures for 1991–1993.

	A	B	C	D	E	F	G	H
1								
2								
3	State	1991	1992	1993	3-Yr Growth			
4	Arkansas	9,743	15,162	25,226	158.91%			
5	Colorado	13,836	21,458	27,345	97.64%			
6	Florida	15,939	28,137	36,831	131.07%			
7	Georgia	48,540	50,915	56,741	16.90%			
8	Indiana	14,022	18,820	32,437	131.33%			
9	Kentucky	12,579	19,556	34,568	174.81%			
10	New York	21,817	37,672	41,901	92.06%			
11	Ohio	24,156	40,107	62,439	158.48%			
12	Oregon	17,968	22,291	34,568	92.39%			
13	Pennsylvania	23,021	24,917	43,813	90.32%			
14	Texas	36,049	43,325	51,574	43.07%			
15	Wyoming	12,336	16,210	23,143	87.61%			
16	*Totals*	250,006	338,570	470,586	88.23%			
17								

Figure 25.1 A sample sheet to chart.

Next, click on the ◪ tool. The ChartWizard will start running, which you can tell because the mouse cursor changes to a crosshair. You are asked to select where you want the chart placed. In this instance, simply select someplace on the sheet outside of the original data table and then click the mouse button.

Now you are asked to verify the range of cells to be included in the chart, as shown in Figure 25.2. Since this matches the range selected earlier, click on the [**Next >**] button to proceed to the next ChartWizard step.

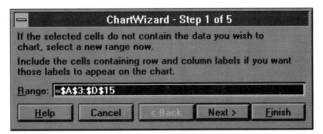

Figure 25.2 The ChartWizard, step 1.

Next you are asked to select a chart type (see Figure 25.3). Select the type of chart you wish to use. Remember, you can also change the chart type later (as you will learn in Lesson 26). For the purposes of this example, accept the default (Column) chart. Click on [**Next >**] to proceed to the next step.

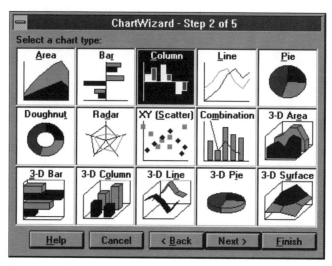

Figure 25.3 *The ChartWizard, step 2, chart types.*

In step 3, you are asked to specify a format for the type of chart you selected (see Figure 25.4). Notice that there are multiple formats available; the exact number will depend on the type of chart you are creating. For the sake of this example you should click on Next > to again accept the default format.

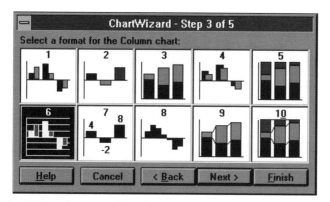

Figure 25.4 *The ChartWizard, step 3, chart format type.*

Now the ChartWizard has enough information to start putting the chart together. You are presented with a sample of what the chart will look like, as shown in Figure 25.5. You are also asked to specify if the data series, axis labels, and legend is correct. In this case it is not correct. Look closely at Figure 25.5, and you will see that the ChartWizard is suggesting that no legend can be derived from the range of cells selected (Use First 0 Rows for Legend Text).

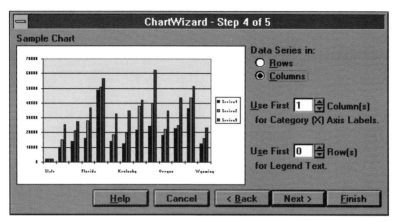

Figure 25.5 *The ChartWizard, step 4, examining the chart.*

This is a common mistake; the legend text should actually be taken from the first row, which specifies the years (these are the column heads in the data table—see Figure 25.1). Since the years are numbers, the ChartWizard assumed they were part of the data and you wanted to chart them. Instead, change the information on this dialog box to indicate you want to use 1 row for legend text. You can do this by either typing a 1 in this field or by clicking on the up arrow to the right of the field. When you have done this, click on the Next > button to proceed to the final step.

As the final step, the ChartWizard asks you what sort of title and labels you want on your chart, as shown in Figure 25.6. You have the opportunity to delete the legend or add a title and axis labels. As you make changes, notice that the sample chart is updated to reflect those changes. When you are satisfied with the changes, click on the Finish button, and the chart is added to your sheet. A sample of a finished chart is shown in Figure 25.7.

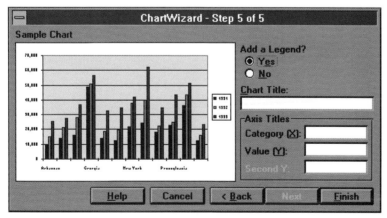

Figure 25.6 *The ChartWizard, step 5, choosing labels.*

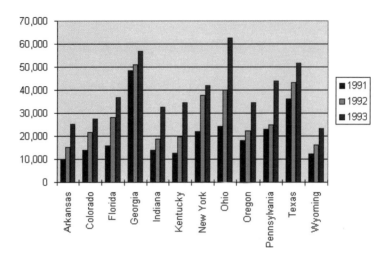

Figure 25.7 An example of a finished embedded chart created with the ChartWizard.

CREATING A CHART SHEET

The other way to create a chart, as a chart sheet, is done in a manner similar to creating an embedded chart. The first step is to select the range of data you want charted. Then, select the Chart option from the Insert menu. You will see the following submenu:

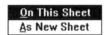

The first choice, On This Sheet, will result in creating an embedded chart, as you learned in the previous section. The second choice, As New Sheet, is the choice you want to make. It starts the ChartWizard, but creates the chart on a brand new sheet, placed immediately before the current sheet.

After you choose this menu choice, the rest of the steps you follow are exactly the same as those described for creating an embedded chart, in the previous section.

> *QUICK REVIEW*
>
> Inserting a chart in your workbook is quick and easy. You can use two types of charts—embedded or a chart sheet. An embedded chart appears within another sheet, while a chart sheet occupies its own sheet.
>
> To create an embedded chart, click on the ChartWizard tool (🔲) on the standard toolbar, or choose Chart from the Insert menu and then choose On This Sheet.
>
> To create a chart sheet, choose Chart from the Insert menu and then choose As New Sheet.
>
> Regardless of whether you are creating an embedded chart or a chart sheet, the ChartWizard leads you through the actual chart creation process.

WHAT YOU NEED TO KNOW

In this lesson you have taken the first steps in mastering the charting capabilities of Excel. This is only the first step, however. You still need to learn how to modify your chart, which is covered in the rest of the lessons in this section.

In this lesson you have learned the following:

☑ A chart is nothing but a graphical representation of the data contained within a sheet.

☑ Excel supports two major types of charts—embedded charts and chart sheets. Embedded charts appear as only a portion of a regular sheet, while a chart sheet fully occupies its own sheet.

☑ Using the ChartWizard greatly simplifies the process of creating charts from existing data.

In the next lesson you will learn how to change the type of chart and how to use AutoFormats for your charts.

Lesson 26

Changing the Chart Type

In Lesson 25 you learned how you can create charts. The examples in that lesson used the default choices proposed by the ChartWizard. This resulted in creating a column chart. Excel, however, supports a wide variety of chart types. In this lesson you will learn how you can modify the type of chart you will be using. You will learn

- Which types of charts are available

- How to change chart types

- How to use chart AutoFormats

- How to create your own AutoFormats

TYPES OF CHARTS

Excel includes 14 different types of charts you can use to represent your data. These 14 types include two-dimensional or three-dimensional versions of the same chart type, as shown in Table 26.1.

Basic Chart Type	2-D Version	3-D Version
Area chart	Area	3-D Area
Bar chart	Bar	3-D Bar
Column chart	Column	3-D Column
Line chart	Line	3-D Line
Pie chart	Pie	3-D Pie
Donut chart	Donut	
Radar chart	Radar	
X-Y chart	XY (Scatter)	
Surface chart		3-D Surface

Table 26.1 Names of various types of charts in Excel.

Note that not all charts have two-dimensional and three-dimensional versions. Besides these 14 major chart types, however Excel also provides variations of each chart type. For instance, there are three different types of bar charts and four different types of 3-D column charts. If you count all the variations, Excel can provide 30 different ways for you to represent your data.

How to Change Chart Types

You might remember from Lesson 25 that you can use the ChartWizard to select the type of chart you want to use. But what if you have already selected a chart type, inserted the chart, and now feel that you need to use a different type of chart? Excel makes changing charts a snap. All you need to do is use the mouse to double-click on the chart. This activates the chart and allows you to make changes to it. (You can tell when an embedded chart is activated because it shows up with a shaded border around it.)

Next, choose the Chart Type option from the Format menu. (If this menu option does not appear, you know that you have not activated the chart.) When you select this option, you will see the Chart Type dialog box, shown in Figure 26.1.

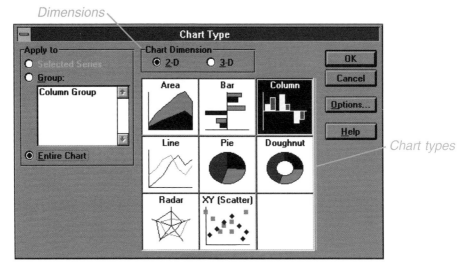

Figure 26.1 *The Chart Type dialog box.*

The current chart type is highlighted, but you can change to any other type of chart you desire. If you want to view the 3-D charts, choose the 3-D radio button at the top of the dialog box.

When you have selected a chart type, you can view the different variations available by clicking on the Options... button. You will then see a dialog box displaying the variations for that type of chart. An example is shown in Figure 26.2.

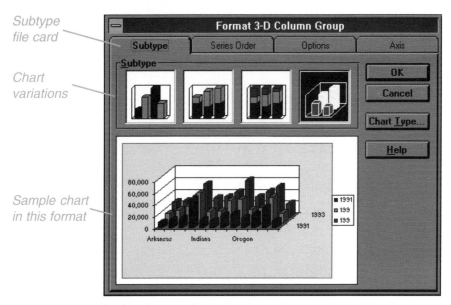

Figure 26.2 Dialog box showing chart type variations.

When you have decided on a chart type and variation, click on the [OK] button, and your chart is reformatted using the chart type and variation you selected. For instance, the chart first presented in Lesson 25 was reformatted as a 3-D column chart; the results are shown in Figure 26.3.

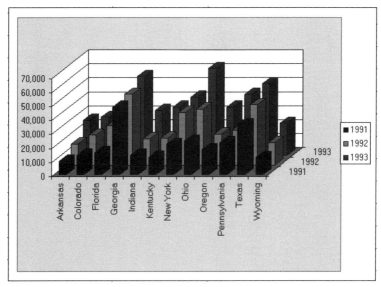

Figure 26.3 An example of a 3-D column chart.

USING AUTOFORMATS FOR CHARTS

Since Excel allows you to change virtually every facet of how your data is graphically presented, the real number of ways it can be shown is almost infinite. (Editing the way your data is presented is covered in Lessons 27 and 28.) In recognition of the many ways data can be represented, Excel includes a chart AutoFormat feature. In some ways this is similar to the AutoFormat first presented in Lesson 20. It differs, however, in that this version of AutoFormat applies only to charts.

To use the AutoFormat feature for charts, activate the chart as described earlier in this lesson. Then choose the AutoFormat option from the Format menu. When you do, you will see the AutoFormat dialog box, shown in Figure 26.4.

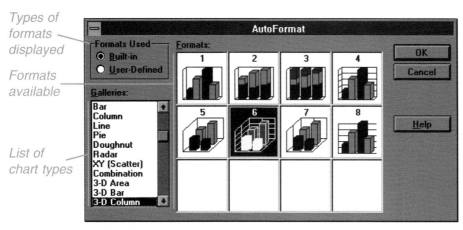

Figure 26.4 The AutoFormat dialog box.

To see which formats are available for various types of charts, select one of the chart types listed in the Galleries list, and then use the up and down arrow keys to select different types. As you do this, you will notice that the formats change. You may also recognize this list from before—it contains the same formats presented in step 3 of the ChartWizard, Lesson 25.

Select a chart type and format to apply and click on OK. Your chart is reformatted to match the format you chose.

CREATING YOUR OWN AUTOFORMATS

There may be times when the built-in AutoFormats just don't meet your needs. In these instances, you can always make changes to your charts following the procedures covered in lessons 27 and 28.

Once you have formatted your chart just the way you want it, you can save all the chart settings as a user-defined AutoFormat. You can then apply these settings to other charts you may create, and you won't have to go through the long or tedious steps necessary to do all the formatting necessary. Instead, you will simply choose an AutoFormat, as described in the previous section.

To create your own AutoFormat, use the different formatting commands to define your chart just the way you want it. Then choose AutoFormat from the Format menu. You will then see the AutoFormat dialog box, as shown earlier in Figure 26.4. Click on the User-Defined radio button in the upper-left corner, and the dialog box will change slightly (there will be more buttons on the right side). Click on the Customize... button. Excel displays the User-Defined AutoFormats dialog box, shown in Figure 26.5.

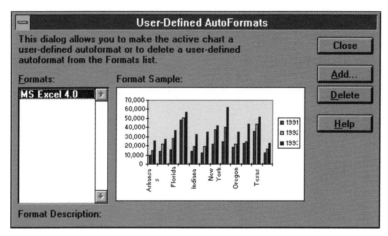

Figure 26.5 *The User-Defined AutoFormats dialog box.*

Click on the Add... button, and you will see the Add Custom AutoFormat dialog box, shown in Figure 26.6. Enter the name and description for that you want assigned to this format and click on OK. The format is saved and is available from the earlier AutoFormat dialog box.

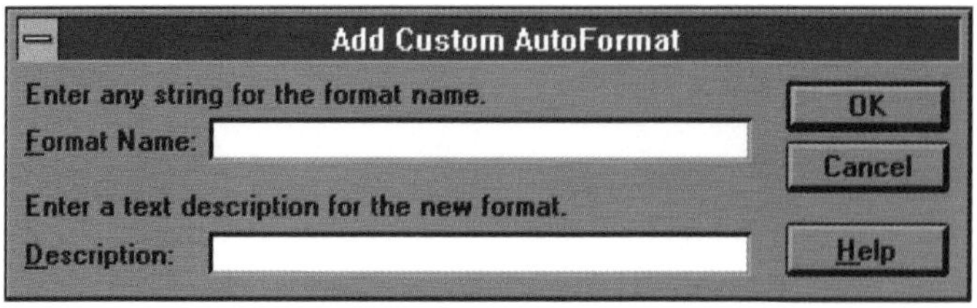

Figure 26.6 *The Add Custom AutoFormat dialog box.*

If you want later to delete a previously defined AutoFormat, choose the [**Delete**] button from the dialog box shown in Figure 26.5. You will be asked to confirm your action, after which the AutoFormat is deleted.

WHAT YOU NEED TO KNOW

You have covered quite a bit of ground in this lesson. You have begun to learn how you can modify the charts you create in Excel. Specifically, you have learned the following:

- ☑ Excel supports 14 different types of charts, including two-dimensional and three-dimensional versions of many charts.

- ☑ Excel provides variations of each chart type. If all the variations are counted, there are over 50 ways you can automatically format your chart.

- ☑ You can quickly and easily change the type of chart used to represent your data. This can be done at any time, and as often as you wish.

- ☑ The quickest way to format a chart is to use the AutoFormat feature for charts.

- ☑ Even though Excel provides quite a few AutoFormat definitions, you can create or delete your own definitions whenever you need to.

In the next lesson you will learn about adding text, titles, and labels to your chart.

Lesson 27

Adding Text to Your Chart

Text is a necessary ingredient of any chart, whether that text indicates values, what the meaning of different parts of the chart are, or titles and legends. Excel can take care of applying many types of text automatically through the use of the ChartWizard, as you undoubtedly discovered in Lesson 25. Other types of text must be added manually. This lesson covers text items you can add to your chart manually. You will learn how to

- Add titles to your chart

- Add data labels to your chart

- Format text in your chart

CHART TITLES

Titles add purpose and meaning to your chart. Excel allows you to add several different types of titles, as shown in Figure 27.1.

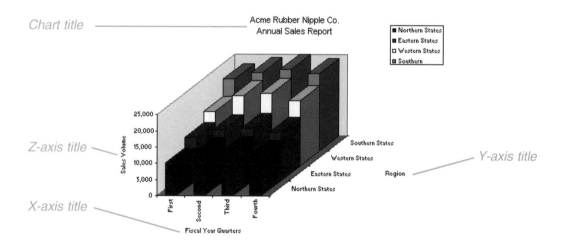

Figure 27.1 Titles on a chart.

The titles that are actually available will vary, depending on the type of chart you are using. For instance, the only type of title available with a pie chart is the chart title itself. Since there are no X, Y, and Z axes on a pie chart, there are not titles available for them.

ADDING TITLES

To insert titles, activate the chart by double-clicking on it (if it is an embedded chart) or by clicking on it once (if it is a chart sheet). Then choose the Titles option from the Insert menu. If this menu option is not available, you will know that you have not fully selected the chart. When you are able to select the Titles option, you will see the Titles dialog box, shown in Figure 27.2.

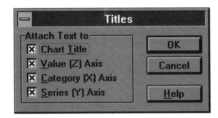

Figure 27.2 The Titles dialog box.

Select the titles you want displayed on the chart (you will not be able to select titles that are impossible to display on the type of chart you are formatting). If an × appears to the left of the title name, then that title will be added to the chart. When you click on OK, the titles will be added to the chart. These titles originally contain dummy text. To change them, you must follow the procedures listed in the following section.

CHANGING TITLE TEXT

To change the text contained within a title, simply click on the title with the mouse cursor. The title is selected and surrounded with a box. When you move the mouse cursor inside the box, it changes to an insertion point. Click the mouse pointer once to edit the text.

Notice that if you press ENTER, the cursor only moves to the next line; you are still adding to the title. To signify that you have finished entering title text, you must use the mouse pointer to select some other part of your chart.

MOVING TITLES

When you add titles to your chart, Excel places them in a position that it feels is best for the title. Thus, an axis title will be centered on the axis. You can move titles very easily, however. To do this, use the mouse to select the title text. When you do, it becomes surrounded with a box:

Selected text

1993 Sales Volume

Use the mouse to point to the border around the title. Press and hold down the mouse button. As you move the mouse, the title is also moved. When you release the mouse button, the title remains at the new location.

QUICK REVIEW

Titles can help add meaning to the information presented in a chart. Excel allows you to add several types of titles to your chart. To add titles, select the chart and choose Titles from the Insert menu. You will see the Titles dialog box, where you can specify which titles you want displayed. Select the check boxes beside the titles you want displayed, and then click on [**OK**]

Once a title is displayed on your chart, you can edit it and move it as you would many other chart items.

ADDING DATA LABELS

Data labels are used to indicate what the main part of the chart represents. Depending on the type of chart you are creating, data labels can mean quite a bit. For instance, if you are formatting a pie chart, the data can be more difficult to understand without data labels. Figure 27.3 shows an example of data labels.

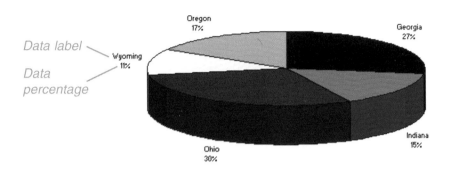

Figure 27.3 Data labels on a chart.

To add data labels, activate the chart by double-clicking on it (if it is an embedded chart) or by clicking on it once (if it is a chart sheet). Then choose the Data Labels option from the Insert menu. You will see the dialog box shown in Figure 27.4.

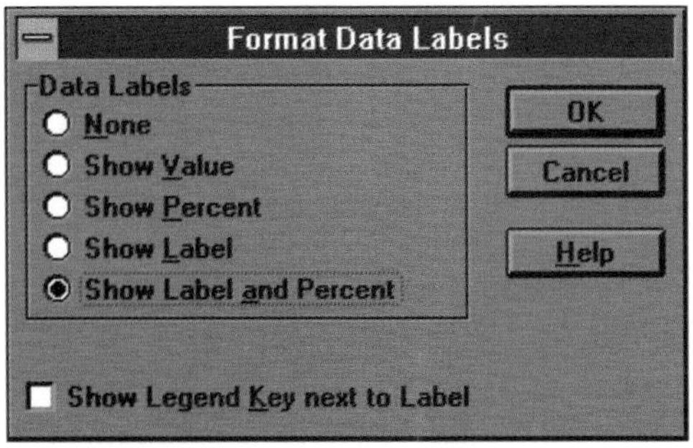

Figure 27.4 The Format Data Labels dialog box.

There are basically three different types of data labels you can choose; some options allow a combination of more than one type. If you look back at Figure 27.3, you will see two of the types displayed. If you choose the Show Value option, your data labels will appear as shown in Figure 27.5.

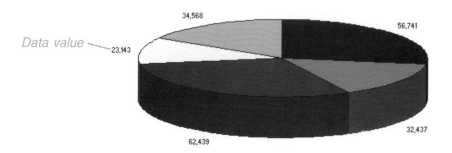

1993 Sales Volume

Figure 27.5 *Data labels after selecting the Show Value option.*

FORMATTING CHART TEXT

You can format any text that appears on your chart by using the mouse to double-click on it. When you do, you will see a dialog box similar to the Format Title dialog box shown in Figure 27.6. The title for the dialog box may change—depending on what it is you are formatting—but the concept is the same.

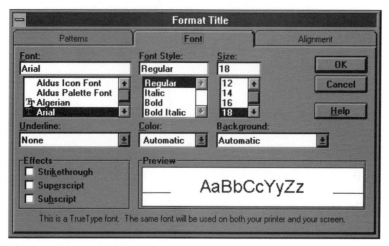

Figure 27.6 *Changing formatting of text in a chart.*

You can change the font and other formatting information for the text much as you would change formatting in cells (see Lesson 15). Notice from Figure 27.6 that you can choose different file cards to change Patterns, which includes colors, and Text Alignment. Again, these use the same techniques as you used when you formatted information in cells.

WHAT YOU NEED TO KNOW

Adding text to your chart and formatting it is a simple matter. Excel allows you to add several types of titles and data labels to help make your charts clearer and more meaningful. In this lesson you have learned

- ☑ Titles are the most common type of text you can add to your chart. The type of titles available for your chart will depend on the type of chart you are using.

- ☑ You can add titles to your chart by first selecting the chart and then choosing the Titles option from the Insert menu.

- ☑ Title text can be changed by first using the mouse to select the title you want to change, and then using the mouse to click at the position within the title where you want to edit the title.

- ☑ Data labels, another common type of chart text, can make the information in your chart more understandable. You add data labels by selecting the chart and then choosing the Data Labels option from the Insert menu.

- ☑ Text within titles or data labels can be formatted by double-clicking on the title or data label you want to format. From the resulting dialog box, make your formatting changes and then click on OK

In the next lesson you will learn how to change the way your chart appears.

Lesson 28

Changing How Your Chart Looks

In Lesson 26 you learned how you can change the type of chart you use to represent your data, and in Lesson 27 you learned how you can add text to your chart. Excel also allows you to change just about every other aspect of your chart, as well. In this lesson you will learn the fundamentals of how to do that. You will learn

- How to change the size of your chart
- How to select items in a chart
- How to change items in the chart
- Which chart items can be changed
- How to change 3-D perspective
- How to undo changes

CHANGING CHART SIZE

If you are working with an embedded chart, you can change the size of the chart to any size you want. You cannot directly change the size of a chart sheet; it is set to be one single page. (You can modify the printed size of the chart, as covered in Lesson 29.)

You change the size of an embedded chart the same as you would any other graphic object. Click once on the chart, and handles will appear around the chart border. As you move the mouse pointer over these handles, they change to sizing arrows:

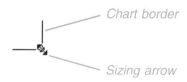

Chart border

Sizing arrow

This example shows what the sizing arrow looks like at the corner of a graphic. The sizing arrow at the side or bottom of a graphic points left and right or up and down, respectively.

To size the graphic, click and hold the left mouse button and drag the border until it is the size you want. The arrow heads point in the direction which you can move the border. When you release the mouse button, the graphic is resized and reformatted.

SELECTING AND CHANGING CHART ITEMS

Before you can change anything in your chart, you must first select it. This is done by using the mouse pointer to point to the item you want to change, and then double-clicking on the left mouse button. This will invariably bring up a dialog box that allows you to change formatting for the item.

Note: There is no other way to access these formatting dialog boxes; only by double-clicking on the item.

What sort of items can you select? In large part that depends on the type of chart you are building. In general, however, you can select just about any part of your chart. For instance, if you point to one of the axes of the chart (X, Y, or Z) and double-click, you will see a Format Axis dialog box similar to the one shown in Figure 28.1.

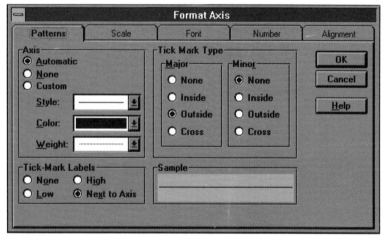

Figure 28.1 The Format Axis dialog box.

Notice, in this example, that you can change virtually every aspect of the axis. It would be repetitive to go through how to change everything that these dialog boxes allow you to change; you have already learned the basics of how to do this earlier in this book. All you need to do is to apply the same principles you learned earlier to this situation, and you will do just fine. When you are through making changes, click on the [OK] button, and the chart is updated to reflect your alterations.

WHICH CHART ITEMS CAN BE CHANGED?

In general, if you can see a chart item displayed, you can change how it is displayed. The types of items displayed will vary, depending on the type of chart you selected. The types of items that can be changed are

- X, Y, or Z axes
- Data series
- Legends
- Chart text

- Plot area
- Chart area
- Gridlines
- Chart walls

Simply select the item as indicated in the previous section, and then make the changes desired.

3-D CHANGES

All of these items discussed so far are selected and formatted with the mouse. In addition, if you are using a 3-D chart, you can choose 3-D View from the Format menu. When you do, you will see the Format 3-D View dialog box, as shown in Figure 28.2.

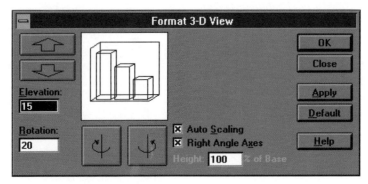

Figure 28.2 The Format 3-D View dialog box.

Using this dialog box, you can change the positioning and relative size of all the 3-D items in the chart. The exact items displayed in the dialog box will vary, depending on the type of 3-D chart you are formatting.

If you prefer, the same effects can be achieved by selecting the chart area with the mouse so that handles appear at all corners of the chart, as shown in Figure 28.3.

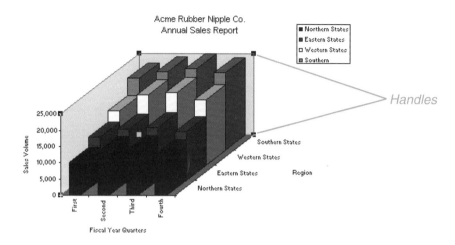

Figure 28.3 A sample 3-D chart, showing the graph selected.

As you move the mouse pointer over one of these handles, it changes to a crosshair. If you click and hold the left mouse button, you can rotate or adjust the entire graphic image using the mouse. When you release the mouse button, the chart is redrawn from the new perspective. Your success in doing this will depend, for the most part, on your precision with the mouse and your ability to envison how you want the 3-D chart displayed. In other words, you may need to play a while with the positioning of the graph before you arrive at the look you want.

UNDOING CHANGES

As with almost any other Excel command, you can undo changes using either the Undo command from the Edit menu or the ⟲ tool from the standard toolbar. This command or tool must be used immediately after the change has been made, however.

If you want to undo an entire series of formatting commands, you should probably close the workbook and reload it from disk. This will start you over with your workbook (and chart) at the condition it was when last saved to disk.

WHAT YOU NEED TO KNOW

Excel allows you to change virtually every aspect of the way your chart is presented. You can change colors, patterns, positioning, and scales easily and quickly. In this lesson you have learned what is capable and how you can apply your knowledge of Excel formatting to charts. You have learned that you can format the charts in much the same way as you formatted information in your sheets. This lesson has taught you the following:

☑ You can change the size of your chart by selecting it and then using the mouse to move the handles which appear around the border of the chart.

☑ Using the mouse, you can select different parts of your chart by clicking on them.

☑ If you double-click on a portion of your chart, you can make changes to that item.

☑ To undo changes to your chart, you can use the Undo option from the Edit menu or the ⟲ tool.

In the next lesson you will learn about printing your chart.

Lesson 29

Printing Your Chart

In Lesson 13 you learned how to print the information contained within your workbook. In this lesson you will take another look at printing, this time focusing on printing charts. In many respects, printing charts is very similar to printing sheets from your workbook. Indeed, you select printers and can use Print Preview in the same way as described in Lesson 13. However, there are other aspects that are dissimilar. In this lesson you will learn how to

- Print an embedded chart
- Prepare a chart sheet for printing
- Send your chart to the printer
- Print a single copy of your chart

PRINTING AN EMBEDDED CHART

Since an embedded chart is included as part of a regular worksheet, you can print one just as you would any other sheet. Thus, the information discussed in Lesson 13 is most pertinent to printing embedded charts. You can also refer to the section entitled "Sending Your Chart to the Printer," later in this lesson.

If you work with multiple charts on the same sheet, however, you will want to pay particular attention to where Excel places page breaks. If the pages do not appear as you want them to, you will need to adjust the size of the charts so they fit on the number of pages desired. Alternatively, if you want everything to fit on one page, you can use the scaling capabilities of Excel (again, described in Lesson 13).

PREPARING A CHART SHEET FOR PRINTING

Chart sheets, on the other hand, take a bit more preparation in order to print. While you can still perform a Print Preview to see how your printed chart will appear, Excel adds a different file card to the Page Setup dialog box to enable you to make modifications for printing.

To modify how a chart sheet appears, select the Page Setup command from the File menu, and make sure you select the Chart file card. The Page Setup dialog box appears, as shown in Figure 29.1.

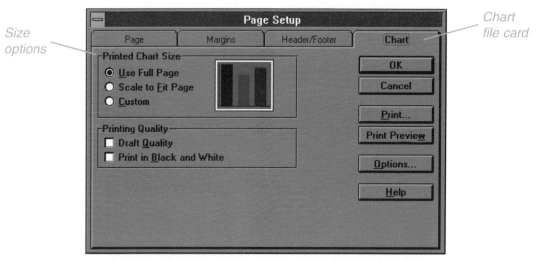

Size options

Chart file card

Figure 29.1 *The Page Setup dialog box, with the Chart file card selected.*

From this dialog box, you can select the quality of the printout, as well as specify how much of the printed page the chart should occupy. Since a chart sheet is, by nature, an entire sheet of paper, the default selection is Use Full Page. You can also choose either of the other options (Scale to Fit Page or Custom) to specify a different page size, however. If you choose either of these options and click on **OK**, Excel places handles around the image, as shown in Figure 29.2.

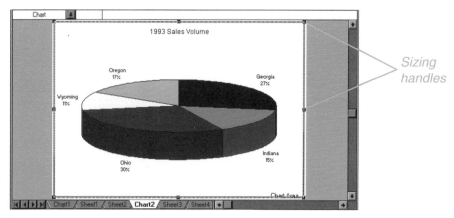

Sizing handles

Figure 29.2 *A chart sheet with sizing handles.*

As you move the mouse pointer over the handles, it changes to sizing arrows. These are the same type of arrows described in Lesson 28. Use the mouse to click on the handles and drag the border of the chart to reflect the size you want to use. The direction of the arrowheads on the sizing arrows will indicate the direction in which you can move the border. When you release the mouse button, the chart is resized and redrawn automatically.

SENDING YOUR CHART TO THE PRINTER

If you are not printing to a color printer, the first thing you will want to do is make sure you use the Print Preview feature to see what your chart will appear like in black and white. If there is not enough contrast between different parts of your chart, you will want to make changes to either the colors or patterns used within the chart so there is a better contrast and your printed chart will look better.

When you are ready to print your chart, you do this by using the Print option from the File menu. You will then see the Print dialog box, as shown in Figure 29.3.

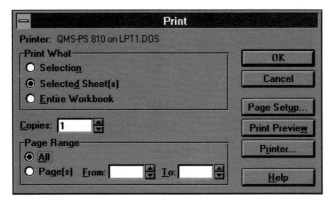

Figure 29.3 The Print dialog box.

This is the same dialog box you learned about in Lesson 13. The information at the top of the dialog box indicates where your chart will be printed. If this is not the printer you want to use, choose a different printer, as described in Lesson 13.

The actual information and options available from the Print dialog box can vary, depending on the type of printer you are using. Different printers have different capabilities, and Windows takes advantage of these capabilities as much as possible. In general, however, you can use this dialog box to select the number of copies you want to print, along with which pages you want to print.

One of the other things you can specify is what you want sent to the printer. This is done making a selection in the Print What box. By default, this field is set to Selected Sheet(s), typically meaning that only the current sheet will be printed. By changing this field, you can also specify that only a Selection be printed or that your entire Workbook is printed. You should note that the Selection option will only be available if you are printing a sheet containing an embedded chart; it is not available when printing a chart sheet.

When you are satisfied with what you want to print, click on the [OK] button or press ENTER. Excel will send your information to the printer, as you have directed.

PRINTING A SINGLE COPY OF YOUR CHART

Many times you will want to print only a single copy of your chart. Excel provides a quick way to do this using the 🖶 tool. When you click on this tool, it is the same as choosing the Print command from the File menu and immediately clicking on [OK].

Using the 🖶 tool results in one copy of your chart being printed. If you need more than one copy, you must either use the Print command as described in the previous section or click on the 🖶 tool multiple times (once for each copy you want to print).

QUICK REVIEW

Printing your chart is, in most instances, just as simple as printing sheets within your workbook. The only exception is if you want to modify how a chart sheet prints. To make these types of modifications, you should choose Page Setup from the File menu, and then make sure the Chart file card is selected.

To print multiple copies of the same chart, or to modify printing options, choose Print from the File menu. To print a single copy of your chart, click on the 🖶 tool on the standard toolbar.

WHAT YOU NEED TO KNOW

Whether it is for a presentation or for a final report, printing is most often the end result of creating a chart. With Excel, it is virtually as easy to print a chart as it is to print other parts of your workbook. In this lesson you have learned the similarities and differences between printing regular workbook information and your charts. You have learned the following:

☑ If you are printing an embedded chart, it is important to use Print Preview so you can make sure the chart will appear on the page as you want it to.

☑ Printing a chart, in general, follows the same process as printing a regular sheet. Printing is accomplished either by choosing Print from the File menu or by clicking on the 🖨 tool.

☑ If you are printing a chart sheet, you can adjust the size of the chart by using the Print Setup option from the File menu, and then selecting the Chart file card.

The next section introduces Excel shortcuts, beginning with toolbars in the next lesson.

Section Six

EXCEL SHORTCUTS

By this point you have learned how to use Excel. Without learning anything else, you could use the program effectively and efficiently for all your number-crunching needs. There are shortcuts, however, which you can use to make your use of Excel even more effective. This section will teach you how to do everything from customizing the toolbars to working with multiple documents and creating short macros. You will even learn how to change how Excel starts, in order to begin using the program quicker. When you get through learning the information in this section, you will know as much as the experts—the only difference will be experience, which comes with time and use.

Lesson 30

Using Toolbars

In Lesson 4 you learned about the two toolbars normally displayed in Excel—the standard and formatting toolbars. In other lessons you have used the tools on these toolbars to perform various functions and complete certain commands. In this lesson you will focus more squarely on the toolbars you can use with Excel. You will learn

- Which toolbars are available
- How to select different toolbars
- How to position toolbars
- How to create your own toolbars
- How to modify toolbars
- How to delete toolbars
- How to reset a toolbar

AVAILABLE TOOLBARS

Excel has 14 different predefined toolbars available for your use. Each toolbar is intended for a different, specific purpose. While you might never use all of the toolbars available, you might use some of them if you find yourself doing tasks for which the toolbars are designed.

Table 30.1 lists the different toolbars available with Excel. You may want to take a look at them so you can become acquainted with what is available.

Toolbar	Tools	Purpose
Auditing	8	Aid in error detection for formulas
Chart	5	Aid in creating charts
Drawing	21	Aid in creating a graphic object

Table 30.1 The toolbars available in Excel. (continued on next page)

Toolbar	Tools	Purpose
Formatting	17	Formatting characters, numbers, and cells
Forms	16	Aid in creating and modifying electronic forms
Full Screen	1	Toggles full-screen display of the sheet
Microsoft	7	Run other Microsoft applications under Windows
Query and Pivot	8	Use pivot tables and manipulate information within them
Standard	22	The most commonly used functions and commands
Stop Recording	1	Stop the macro recorder
TipWizard	2	Display tips about what you are doing in Excel
Visual Basic	12	Create Visual Basic modules
WorkGroup	6	Access network-related programs

Table 30.1 *The toolbars available in Excel. (continued from previous page)*

HOW TO SELECT DIFFERENT TOOLBARS

For the most part, Excel does not display different toolbars automatically as they are needed. Instead, it is left to your discretion to determine when you need a toolbar. Thus, it is important to understand what is available (see the previous section) so you can make an informed decision about when you should use a certain toolbar.

There are two ways you can access some toolbars and only one way to access others. Some toolbars can be displayed by using tools existing on other toolbars. For instance, there are two other toolbars you can access from the standard toolbar. If you click on ⬚, you will see the drawing toolbar. Likewise, if you click on ⬚, you will see the TipWizard toolbar.

The other method of displaying toolbars is to use the Toolbars option from the View menu. When you click on this option, you will see the Toolbars dialog box, shown in Figure 30.1.

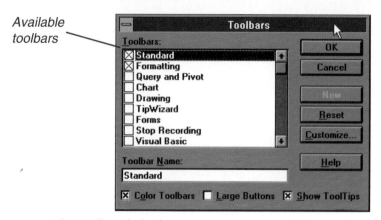

Available toolbars

Figure 30.1 *The Toolbars dialog box.*

To turn a toolbar on, make sure the check box associated with the toolbar is selected. Then, when you click on | OK |, you will see the toolbar appear.

POSITIONING AND CONTROLLING TOOLBARS

Toolbars in Excel can assume two positions on your screen—floating or docked. You can move a *floating* toolbar anywhere around your screen; it exists within its own window. Figure 30.2 shows an example of the Microsoft toolbar, which starts as a floating toolbar.

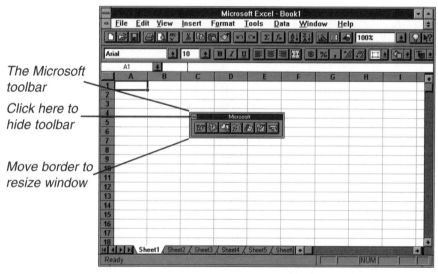

The Microsoft toolbar

Click here to hide toolbar

Move border to resize window

Figure 30.2 *The Microsoft toolbar, floating in the middle of the document window.*

Notice that the toolbar just floats in the middle of the sheet. You can move and size the toolbar window as you would any other window (see Lesson 3). If you want to hide the toolbar, you can click on the tiny control button in the upper-left corner of the toolbar window.

The other position for a toolbar is *docked.* This means you can attach the toolbar to the sides of the program window, much as the standard and formatting toolbars are positioned. To dock a floating toolbar, simply move it so it is positioned near the top or sides of the program window. Figure 30.3 shows an example of the Microsoft toolbar docked at the left of the Excel program window.

The Microsoft toolbar

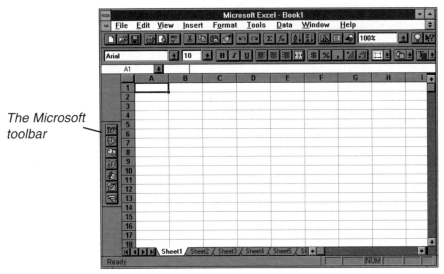

Figure 30.3 The Microsoft toolbar, docked at the left of the program window.

Notice that the toolbar no longer appears in its own window. To change it back to a floating toolbar, double-click on the toolbar background.

CREATING TOOLBARS

Using Excel, you can create your own custom toolbars that contain only the tools you want to use. To do this, select the Toolbars option from the View menu. You will see the Toolbars dialog box, shown earlier in Figure 30.1. In the Toolbar Name field, type the name you want assigned to your toolbar (do not use the same name as any of the existing toolbars). Then click on the ▭ New ▭ button, and you will see an empty, floating toolbar appear on the screen. You will also see the Customize dialog box, shown in Figure 30.4.

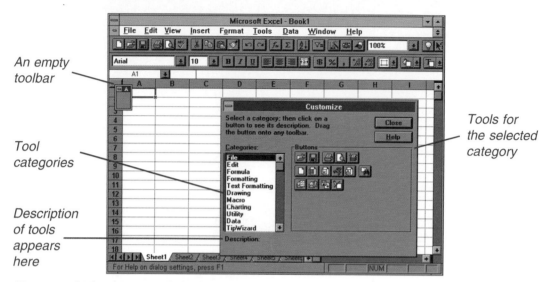

An empty toolbar

Tool categories

Description of tools appears here

Tools for the selected category

Figure 30.4 *The Customize dialog box and a new toolbar.*

To add tools to the new toolbar, select a tool category from the list in the Customize dialog box. As you do this, the available tools will change. Next, click on one of the available tool buttons. If the description at the bottom of the Customize dialog box reflects what you want to do with the tool, then drag the tool button to your toolbar. If there are already other buttons on the new toolbar, make sure you drop the new tool at the position where you want it to appear on the toolbar. If you position a tool in the wrong place, you can always move them around by dragging them to where you want them positioned.

You can add as many tools to your new toolbar as you desire. Figure 30.5 shows our newly created toolbar after a few tools have been added to it. When you click on the [**Close**] button, the Customize dialog box disappears, and your changes are saved.

To add tools to the new toolbar, select a tool category from the list in the Customize dialog box. Then, click on one of the available tool buttons. If the description at the bottom of the Customize dialog box reflects what you want to do with the tool, then drag the tool button to your toolbar. Figure 30.5 shows our newly created toolbar after a few tools have been added to it.

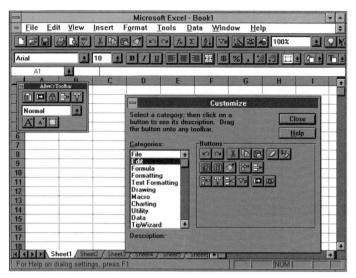

Figure 30.5 *The new toolbar after adding a few tools.*

When you click on the ⬛ Close button, the Customize dialog box disappears, and your changes are saved.

Note: It's perfectly fine if a tool you want to add to a custom toolbar is already on an existing toolbar. A tool can exist on multiple bars.

CHANGING TOOLBARS

Excel provides you with the capability to modify toolbars so they contain the tools you want to use. You can edit your own toolbars (created according to the procedures in the previous section) or you can edit Excel's built-in toolbars.

To change a toolbar, first make sure that the toolbar you want to modify is displayed. Then select the Toolbars option from the View menu. You will see the Toolbars dialog box, shown earlier in Figure 30.1. Click on the Customize... button, and the Customize dialog box appears (previously shown in Figure 30.4). You can now perform any of the following functions:

- To add a tool, select the tool category and drag the desired button to the place you want the tool on the toolbar.

- To remove a tool, select the tool on the toolbar and drag it off the toolbar.

- To move a tool, drag it to the new position on the toolbar.

- To resize a drop-down list, drag the left or right side of the list box to make it larger or smaller.

When you are done modifying your toolbars, click on the [Close] button. The Customize dialog box disappears and your changes are saved.

RESETTING AND DELETING TOOLBARS

If you want to return one of the built-in toolbars to its unmodified condition, choose the Toolbars option from the View menu. When you see the Toolbars dialog box, shown earlier in Figure 30.1, select the toolbar you want to reset. Then click on the [Reset] button. The toolbar is immediately changed back to the unmodified state.

If you select a custom toolbar, the [Reset] button changes to a [Delete] button. If you click this button, you are asked to confirm your selection (as depicted in Figure 30.6). If you click on [OK], the toolbar is deleted.

Figure 30.6 *This confirmation dialog box appears when you delete a custom toolbar.*

Note: *Once you delete a toolbar, there is no way to recover it. You can only create the toolbar again.*

WHAT YOU NEED TO KNOW

Toolbars are an important shortcut in Excel. They allow you to perform commands and functions faster than you could through using the menus—often faster than remembering and using the shortcut keys. In this lesson you have learned how you can control the toolbars to reflect the work you want to perform. You have learned the following items:

☑ Excel contains 14 different toolbars, each of which can be used to accomplish different purposes.

☑ To control which toolbars are displayed, choose the Toolbars option from the View menu.

☑ You can use the mouse to move toolbars around the screen or to change the size of a toolbar.

☑ Toolbars can either float (be positioned over the top of other screen items) or be docked (appear at the edge of the Excel program window).

☑ You can easily create your own custom toolbars by choosing Toolbars from the View menu, entering a name for the toolbar, and then clicking on the New button.

☑ Existing toolbars (including those provided with Excel) can be changed by choosing Toolbars from the View menu, selecting the toolbar you want to change, and then clicking on the Customize... button.

☑ If you create a custom toolbar, you can later delete it. If you modify a built-in toolbar, you can later reset it to its default condition.

In the next lesson you will learn how panes can save you pain by allowing you to work with different parts of the same workbook.

Lesson 31

Working with Different Parts of the Same Workbook

As you begin to work with larger and larger sheets in Excel, you will find there are times you need to refer simultaneously to information located in different parts of your sheet. For instance, you may be developing some summary information based on detail provided earlier in the sheet. If the information you need to refer to cannot appear on the screen at the same time, it can be bothersome to flip back and forth to refer to the information.

Fortunately, Excel provides a quick and simple way to look at different parts of the same sheet. In this lesson you will learn

- What panes are

- How to open a pane

- How you can control the size of panes

- How you can switch between panes

- How to close a pane

WHAT ARE PANES?

A *pane* is simply a different view of a single sheet. This differs, however, from the views discussed in Lesson 24. Excel allows you to use panes so you can view two different parts of the same sheet at the same time. You can open a pane by using one of the pane bars. These are thick, short bars located at the top of the vertical scroll bar or at the right side of the horizontal scroll bar:

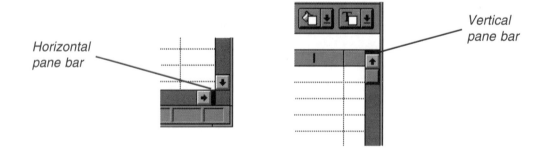

Horizontal
pane bar

Vertical
pane bar

When you move the mouse cursor over the top of one of these bars, it changes to indicate you can grab the bar:

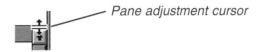

Pane adjustment cursor

If you click and hold down the left mouse button, you can drag the pane bar to indicate how you want the window split. When you release the mouse button, the window is split in two. You can split the window both horizontally and vertically, resulting in four different panes, as shown in Figure 31.1.

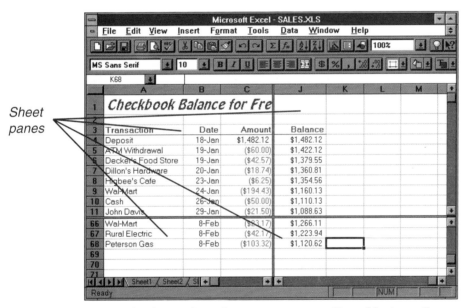

Sheet panes

Figure 31.1 An example of a window split into panes, vertically and horizontally.

You can also use the mouse to double-click on a pane bar. Excel will the divide the document window in half automatically, in the direction appropriate for the pane bar you selected. Thus, if you double-click on the horizontal pane bar, the window is split in half horizontally.

You can also split a document window into panes by using the Split option from the Window menu. Using this option splits the window in half both horizontally and vertically. You can then adjust the position of the dividers by using the mouse, as described in the following section.

CONTROLLING THE SIZE OF PANES

Once you have divided the workbook window into different panes, you can control the size of each pane by using the pane bar. Again, move the mouse cursor over the bar. As you do, the cursor changes shape again. You can click and hold down the left mouse button, which grabs the bar. As you move the mouse, the pane bar moves, as well. When you release the mouse button, the window is divided at the point where you released the mouse button.

QUICK REVIEW

Through the use of panes, you can view different parts of a sheet at the same time. To open a pane, you can do any of the following:

- Use the mouse to drag a pane bar to where you want the window split.

- Double-click on a pane bar to split the window in half.

- Choose the Split option from the Window menu.

Once panes are open, you can change their size by using the mouse to drag the appropriate pane bar to a new location.

JUMPING BETWEEN PANES

Each pane in a window is independent of the other. You can move from one pane to the other by simply using the mouse. Point into one pane and click the mouse button, and that pane becomes active. If you want to move to another pane, use the mouse cursor to point to the other pane. When you click the mouse button, that pane becomes active. If you would rather not keep grabbing the mouse to switch between panes, you can use the **F6** key. Pressing this key will switch between the panes on the screen.

Notice that the text in each pane can be scrolled independently. The two possible horizontal panes have their own vertical scroll bars. Similarly, the two possible vertical panes have their own horizontal scroll bars. If this seems confusing, take a look at Figure 31.2.

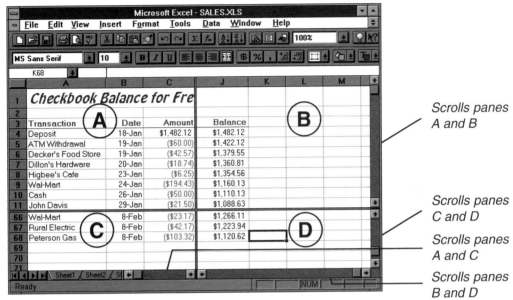

Figure 31.2 *How the scroll bars affect different panes.*

You should realize that, no matter how many panes you use (two or four), these only represent different places in the same sheet. If you make changes in one pane, they are automatically made in the others.

CLOSING A PANE

One of the drawbacks to working with panes is that you cannot see as much of the sheet as you could if you weren't using panes. Thus, you will probably want to close the panes when you have finished whatever you needed them for.

To close a pane, simply double-click on the appropriate pane bar. When you do, the pane bar moves back to its original position, either to the top of the vertical scroll bar or to the right of the horizontal scroll bar.

There are other ways you can close panes, as well. For instance, if you want to return to a full view of the sheet and remove all panes at once, you can choose the Remove Split option from the Window menu. You can also close a pane by using the mouse to move a pane bar off the screen.

WHAT YOU NEED TO KNOW

Workbook panes can be used to view different parts of the sheet on which you are working. If you find yourself jumping back and forth between two locations in a sheet quite a bit, you should divide the document window into panes so you can work on both parts of the workbook at once.

In this lesson you should have learned the following:

☑ Excel allows you to divide a document window into panes. These panes allow you to view two different parts of the same sheet.

☑ Each pane can be scrolled independently of the others in either a horizontal or vertical direction.

☑ The size of panes can be changed by using the mouse to move the pane bar to a new position, horizontally or vertically.

☑ The easiest way to move between panes is to use the mouse to select a cell or other item within the pane you want to use. You can also switch between panes by pressing the **F6** key.

☑ To close a pane, you use the mouse to double-click on the pane bar or choose the Remove Split option from the Window menu.

In addition to working with more than one view of a workbook in a given session, Excel allows you to open more than one workbook, which you will learn in the next lesson.

Lesson 32

Working with More Than One Workbook

In Lesson 31 you learned how you can divide your Excel document window into individual panes, which allow you to view different parts of the same sheet. But what if you want to work with multiple workbooks, not with just one? Excel also allows you to do this quickly and easily. In this lesson you will learn how to

- Open multiple workbooks
- Jump between different workbook windows
- View more than one workbook window at a time

OPENING MULTIPLE WORKBOOKS

In Lesson 12 you learned how to load a workbook. Since that time, you have been working with only one workbook at a time. However, Excel will allow you to open more than one workbook at a time. Each workbook has its own workbook window, which you can switch between.

For instance, let's assume you are working on the month-end statistics for your business. This is a sheet that you prepare on a monthly basis, each month having its own workbook. Since Excel allows you to have more than one workbook open at a time, you can have both this month's report and last month's report open at the same time. This allows you the potential of easily comparing this month's statistics to those of last month. Later in this lesson you will learn how you can even view both files at once.

To open multiple workbooks, just open them as you would your original workbook. You can use any of the techniques described in Lesson 12. There is another way to open multiple workbooks, however. Excel will allow you to open multiple copies of the *same workbook*. This is done by choosing the New Window option from the Window menu. If you do this, notice that Excel changes the filename that appears in the title bar. It appends a colon and a window number after the filename, as shown here:

Microsoft Excel - SALES.XLS:2

In this instance, Excel has appended a colon and a 2, indicating that this is the second window for this file. You can work in either window you want; the changes you make in one are automatically reflected in the other.

JUMPING BETWEEN WORKBOOK WINDOWS

To change from one window to the other, use the Window menu. When you pull down this menu, you will see a list of workbook windows available. These appear at the bottom of the menu, as shown in Figure 32.1.

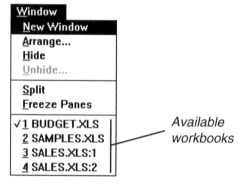

Figure 32.1 Using the Window menu to select a workbook to display.

The currently active workbook window is marked with a check mark. You can select a different window by clicking on the workbook name with the mouse. You can also switch between workbook windows by pressing CTRL-F6. This key combination will cycle you forward through the workbook windows. You can cycle back by pressing SHIFT-CTRL-F6. If you have several workbook windows open, you will probably find it easier to use the menu than to cycle through the windows with the keyboard.

VIEWING MORE THAN ONE WORKBOOK AT A TIME

Besides allowing you to open multiple workbooks, Excel also allows you to adjust the size of the workbook windows. This is done in much the same way as when you use individual windows in the Windows operating system. In Excel, as in Windows, you can adjust window sizes so you can see more than one workbook window at a time. The quickest way to do this is to select the Arrange option from the Window menu. Doing this will display the Arrange Windows dialog box, shown in Figure 32.2

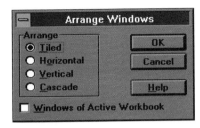

Figure 32.2 *The Arrange Windows dialog box.*

Here you can select any of four different ways to arrange your screen. The Windows of Active Workbook option at the bottom of the dialog box causes Excel to perform any arrangement using only the windows you have opened for the current workbook. (Remember, you learned earlier in this lesson how to use the New Window command to create a duplicate window of the current workbook.) The arrangement option you select will depend, in large part, on the type of data that is contained in your workbook windows. This will be come obvious as you take a look at an example of how each option arranges the screen.

If you select the Tiled option, Excel divides the program window into as many pieces as necessary to display all the open workbooks. Thus, if you have two workbooks loaded, your screen is divided in half. Figure 32.3 shows an example of a tiled window with four workbooks loaded.

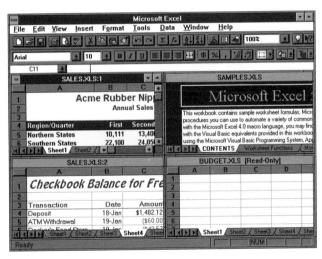

Figure 32.3 *Four tiled windows in Excel.*

The Horizontal option results in the workbook windows being tiled horizontally in the available screen space. Figure 32.4 shows an example of how your screen might appear after choosing this option.

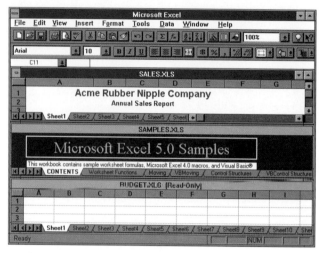

Figure 32.4 *Horizontally arranged windows in Excel.*

The Vertical option is the opposite of the Horizontal option. Using this option results in the workbook windows being tiled vertically across the screen. Figure 32.5 shows an example of your screen after using this option.

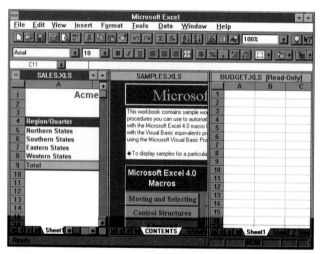

Figure 32.5 *Vertically arranged windows in Excel.*

Finally, the Cascade option arranges the workbook windows on top of each other, but just a bit off center. This allows you to see all the title bars for the available workbooks, but to only see the sheet area of one workbook. Figure 32.6 shows an example of using the Cascade option.

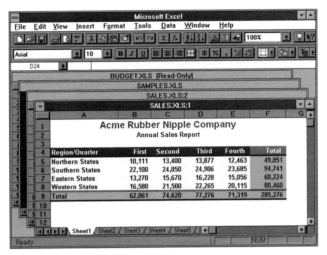

Figure 32.6 *Cascaded windows in Excel.*

WHAT YOU NEED TO KNOW

Excel is a powerful spreadsheet program that allows you to work on multiple workbooks simultaneously. This is done by simply opening the workbooks on which you want to work. In this lesson you have learned these key items:

☑ Using any of the techniques described in Lesson 12, you can open more than one workbook at a time.

☑ To open multiple copies of the same workbook, use the New Window option from the Window menu.

☑ To quickly view more than one workbook on the screen at the same time, select the Arrange option from the Window menu.

☑ You can use the mouse to size workbook windows the same as you would any other window within Excel.

☑ The easiest way to switch between workbook windows is to use the mouse to select a cell or other object in the window containing the workbook you want to work on. You can also, however, select the workbook's file name from the bottom of the Window menu.

In the next lesson you will learn about one of the truly powerful features of Excel; automating frequently used series of commands or key presses with macros.

Lesson 33

Creating Short Macros

Excel includes a full-featured macro command language that allows you to create your own commands. This language is built upon the macro language that has been with Excel for the last several versions. With the release of Excel 5.0 for Windows, however, Excel now also contains facilities to use Visual Basic to create macros. Taken together, these two languages provide you with an enormous amount of power and flexibility.

This lesson will not cover everything there is to know about Excel's macro language, nor will it cover how to use Visual Basic. That amount of detail would take far more space than is available in this entire book. (Indeed, you could use an entire book just about how to use the macro language.) In this lesson you will learn the following, however:

- What a macro is

- How to record short macros

- Where macros are stored

- How to run a macro

- What else you can do with macros

- Where you can get more information

HOW TO RECORD A MACRO

A *macro*, like a small computer program, is a series of instructions, all called with one name. There are two ways you can create Excel macros. The first is to record them using the macro recorder. The other way is to write them from scratch using the macro editor. The latter method of writing macros is beyond the scope of this book, so the discussion here will focus on the first method.

Anything you do in Excel that is of a repetitive nature is a good candidate for a macro. For instance, if you find yourself repeatedly formatting sheets in a certain way, you can consolidate several steps into a single macro. As an example, you could create a macro to do the following:

1. Select the entire sheet

2. Change the font used in the sheet

3. Change the default column width

4. Set up the page format to what is required by your company

5. Move to the first cell in the sheet

6. Save the workbook

If you had to do these six steps manually, you could expend a lot to time and energy over numerous repetitions. If you were to record these steps in a macro, however, you could just let Excel do the work—all you do is issue one command.

To record a macro, choose the Record Macro option from the Tools menu. You will then see a submenu:

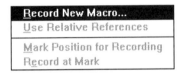

Choose the Record New Macro option and you will see the Record New Macro dialog box, as shown in Figure 33.1.

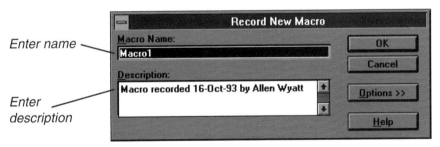

Figure 33.1 The Record New Macro dialog box.

Here you can specify two things. In the Macro Name field, you provide a name you want used for this macro. You can accept the default name, if you desire, but if you plan on using the macro more than once or twice, you will want to use a more descriptive name.

In the Description box, at the bottom on the dialog box, you can optionally provide a comment about your macro. This can come in helpful if you want to remember later what the macro is for.

If you click on the [Options >>] button, you can specify other options for your macro. This displays the expanded Record New Macro dialog box, as shown in Figure 33.2.

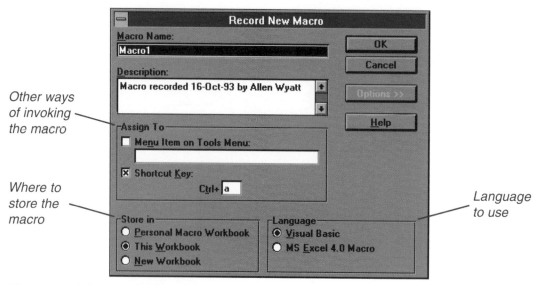

Other ways of invoking the macro

Where to store the macro

Language to use

Figure 33.2 *The expanded Record New Macro dialog box.*

In the Store In box at the bottom of the dialog box, you can specify where you want the macro stored. At the bottom-right corner of the dialog box, you specify what language you want Excel to use when recording this macro.

In the middle of the dialog box is an area where you can indicate whether you want the macro assigned to a menu or the keyboard. You don't have to assign it to one of these, but you can if you desire. For instance, you could assign the macro to CTRL-T combination on the keyboard or another combination that you desire.

If you choose to assign the macro to a menu choice, you should supply the name that will be used on the Tools menu to run this macro.

Once you click on the [OK] button, Excel displays the stop recording toolbar (see Lesson 30) and starts recording everything you do. The stop recording toolbar look like this:

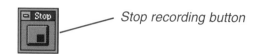

Stop recording button

Once this toolbar appears, you should start going through the steps you want the macro to perform. In the example provided earlier, you would start doing the six steps manually. When you have finished with the steps you want in the macro, click on the stop button (the only button) from the stop recording toolbar. The macro is then saved and available for use at any time.

HOW TO RUN A MACRO

There are two ways you can run a macro. If you defined a keypress or menu option you can use to start the macro, then one of those options is the quickest way to invoke it. For instance, if you assigned your macro to CTRL-T, pressing those keys will start executing the steps you recorded in the macro.

The other way to run a macro is to select the Macro option from the Tools menu. When you do, you will see the Macro dialog box, similar to the one in Figure 33.3.

List of available macros

Macro description

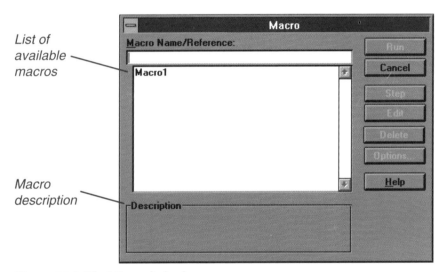

Figure 33.3 *The Macro dialog box.*

The defined macros are shown in the list at the left of the dialog box. You can select a macro from those in the list and then click on the Run button. The macro is executed immediately.

Other Macro Capabilities

Macros can be used to do just about anything you want. The only real limit is your imagination and your knowledge of how to use the macro language. After you record your first macros, you can later edit them using the macro editor. To do this, display the Macro dialog box, as shown earlier in Figure 33.3. In the list of macros displayed, select the one you want to edit, and then click on the ▭ Edit ▭ button. This displays the macro on its own sheet, an example of which is shown in Figure 33.4. Even though this appears just like another sheet in your workbook, notice that there are now rows and columns. Instead, this is a full-featured macro editor which allows you to make changes to your macro as you desire.

Figure 33.4 An example of the macro editor.

A full description of how the macro editor works is beyond the scope of this book. Editing macros requires additional information about what the macro language commands and keywords are. (For information on where you can obtain additional information, see the following section).

Once you have defined your macros, you can then do other things with them, such as assigning the macro to a toolbar tool or adding a menu option that runs the macro. In fact, you can use macros to completely customize the menu structure and toolbar used in Excel.

Once you have defined your macros, you then do other things with them, such as assigning the macro to a toolbar tool or adding a menu option that runs the macro. In fact, you can use macros to completely customize the menu structure and toolbar used in Excel.

WHERE YOU CAN GET MORE INFORMATION

There have been entire books written on the topic of developing Excel macros. If you want more information on this topic, you should refer to any of the following:

- The Reference Information online help (from the Help menu)
- The Programming with Visual Basic online help (from the Help menu)
- *Visual Basic User's Guide,* provided with Excel by Microsoft Corporation
- *Success with Excel for Windows,* by Allen L. Wyatt, Jamsa Press, 1993

WHAT YOU NEED TO KNOW

This lesson has provided you with the briefest possible introduction to Excel macros. You have learned the following:

- ☑ Macros are nothing but a series of actions and commands which can be later repeated by simply running the macro. It is, in effect, a small computer program.

- ☑ Excel provides a built-in macro recorder that allows you to easily create macros by simply doing the action one time.

- ☑ Macros can be assigned to either a menu item, a shortcut key, or a toolbar icon. You can later run the macro by choosing any of these items.

- ☑ To run a macro directly, choose the Macro option from the Tools menu. Then choose the name of the macro and click on the [Run] button.

- ☑ There are many capabilities you can add to a macro if you learn the macro language. While this is beyond the scope of this book, there are many good resources available to help in this learning process.

Perhaps the best way to learn more about macros is to begin using them. Identify some simple tasks that you want to use macros for and then record them. As you work with them more and more, you will become more confident and you can customize Excel to reflect truly the way you work.

In the next lesson you will learn how to customize the way in which Excel starts.

Lesson 34

Changing How Excel Starts

At the very first of this book you learned how to start Excel. In Lesson 1 you learned that you start Excel by double-clicking on the Excel icon in the Program Manager. While this is the most direct way to begin the program, there are other ways you can change how Excel starts. In this lesson you will learn a few of those ways, including how to

- Start Excel with no workbook

- Start Excel with a specific workbook

- Start Excel whenever you start Windows

STARTING WITH NO WORKBOOK

Normally, when you start Excel, it starts with a fresh workbook open, ready for you to start entering information. To many people this is a waste of time, because they normally begin working on existing workbooks instead of starting a new one.

You can configure Excel to start with no workbook. This is done not from within Excel, but from the Program Manager. The first step is to select the Excel program icon by clicking on it with the mouse. Don't double-click on it; that will start the program. Simply highlight the Excel icon.

Next, using the Program Manager menus, choose Properties from the File menu. You will see the Program Item Properties dialog box, shown in Figure 34.1.

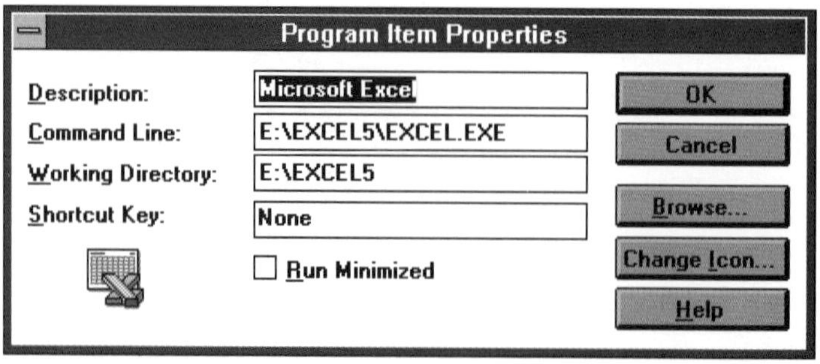

Program Item Properties		
Description:	Microsoft Excel	OK
Command Line:	E:\EXCEL5\EXCEL.EXE	Cancel
Working Directory:	E:\EXCEL5	
Shortcut Key:	None	Browse...
	☐ **Run Minimized**	Change Icon...
		Help

Figure 34.1 The Program Item Properties dialog box.

Notice the second field is labeled *Command Line.* This is the actual operating system command necessary to run Excel. Select this field and move the cursor to the very right side of the command line. The command line should end with the Excel program name, which is EXCEL.EXE. Change the command line so it looks like this:

```
E:\EXCEL5\EXCEL.EXE  /E
```

The DOS path provided to the left of EXCEL.EXE may be different on your system than what is shown here. That's OK; it just means that your Excel program is stored in a different place than mine. The important change here is to add the /E after the program name. This instructs Excel to start with no workbook.

Once you have finished making the changes to the Command Line field, click on the [OK] button. When you later start Excel, there will be no empty workbook waiting for you to start typing. Instead, you will need to open a workbook file explicitly.

STARTING WITH A SPECIFIC WORKBOOK

You can also instruct Excel to start with a particular workbook already loaded. This process is similar to the one described in the last section. Instead of adding the /E to the command line, you will add a filename. For instance, if you wanted Excel to always start with a file called BUDGET.XLS loaded, your command line would be:

```
E:\EXCEL5\EXCEL.EXE  BUDGET.XLS
```

You can also direct Excel to open the file as read-only, if you include /R on the command line. Using the previous example, you would specify this switch in this manner:

```
E:\EXCEL5\EXCEL.EXE  /R  BUDGET.XLS
```

You can use any other filename you desire, however you should remember to use a full pathname if the file is not located in the same directory as Excel.

If you have multiple workbooks you want opened when you start Excel, all you need to do is save them in a special Excel startup directory. Any files you save in the XLSTART directory will be loaded when you start Excel. This directory is located within the directory to which you installed Excel. On my system this would be E:\EXCEL5\XLSTART. Yours will probably be different, but should not be difficult to find.

SETTING A DEFAULT DIRECTORY

If you store your Excel workbooks in a particular location on your hard drive, you may find it valuable to set a default directory where Excel will always look for your files. This is done in one of two ways. The first way is to change the Excel command line, as you did in the previous two sections. This time, however, you use the /P switch, along with a directory. For instance, the following command line would instruct Excel to use D:\EXLDATA as the data directory:

```
E:\EXCEL5\EXCEL.EXE  /P  D:\EXLDATA
```

You can still override this default directory whenever you load or save workbooks; this just sets a starting directory.

The second way to specify a default directory is using the Program Item Properties dialog box, as shown earlier in Figure 34.1. Take another look at the figure, noticing that the third is labeled *Working Directory*. If you change this field so it represents your data directory, then Excel will use that directory as a starting place for your files.

QUICK REVIEW

Everyone seems to have their own scheme for where and how they save files. You can get at those files quickly by changing where Excel first looks for files, or by changing the file that Excel starts with.

To change the default directory used by Excel, you can change the Working Directory field maintained by the Program Manager (in Windows; outside of Excel), or you can add the /D switch to the command line that starts Excel program.

To change the file loaded when Excel first starts, add the name of the file to the command line used to start Excel. If you don't want Excel to use any file, use the /E switch on the command line.

STARTING EXCEL WHEN YOU START WINDOWS

If you use Excel a lot, you will probably want to have it always available to use. This is most easily done by starting Excel whenever you start Windows. To do this, you simply need to have the Excel icon in the Startup program group. This can be done by moving the Excel program icon to the Startup group, but this might not be a good idea. Most people who configure

Windows to automatically start Excel move only a copy of the Excel icon to the Startup program group. In this way they will always know that they can also start Excel from their Excel program group, if necessary.

There are two ways you can create a copy of the Excel icon. The first is to use the Program Manager's Copy command, and the second is to use the mouse. To create a copy of the Excel icon using the Copy command, open the Excel program group. Select the Excel program icon by clicking on it with the mouse. Don't double-click on it; that will start the program. Simply highlight the Excel icon.

Next, choose the Copy option from the File menu in the Program Manager. You will see the Copy Program Item dialog box, as shown in Figure 34.2.

Figure 34.2 The Copy Program Item dialog box.

In the To Group field, specify the Startup group. When you click on OK, the program item (the Excel program icon) is copied to the Startup group.

To copy the Excel icon with the mouse, make sure both the Excel icon and the Startup group (either icon or open window) are both visible on the screen. Hold down the CTRL key, point the mouse cursor at the Excel icon, hold down the left mouse button and drag a copy of the icon over on top of the Startup group. Release the mouse button, and the icon will be copied into the group.

Now select the Excel program icon in the Startup group. Again, don't double-click on it; that will start the program. Simply highlight the icon.

Now choose Properties from the File menu in the Program Manager. You will see the Program Item Properties dialog box, shown earlier in Figure 34.1. Make sure the check box labeled Run Minimized is selected, and then click on the OK button. This ensures that when Excel starts, it will be automatically minimized as an icon at the bottom of the Windows desktop.

WHAT YOU NEED TO KNOW

There are many ways you can start Excel. In this lesson you have learned of some changes you can make that affect how you start your session with Excel. You have learned how to

- ☑ Excel is started through Windows by issuing a command to run the program. This command line is maintained by the Program Manager.

- ☑ You can start Excel with no workbook by using the /E switch on the command line.

- ☑ Including a workbook name on the command line results in that workbook being loaded whenever Excel is started.

- ☑ Using the /P switch on the command line results in setting the default directory used by Excel. You can also specify the working directory directly within the Program Manager.

- ☑ You can start Excel automatically whenever Windows starts by moving or copying the Excel program item icon to the Startup program group.

By combining the starting methods in this lesson, you can get to work quicker and easier.

By now you have completed all the lessons in this book, and you are no longer a beginner in Excel—you are on your way to becoming an Excel expert. By applying the concepts you have learned here, you will quickly become proficient in even the most esoteric of Excel functions. Good luck in all your learning efforts.

Index